GOING

STRONG

GOING

STRONG

BY

PAT YORK

Arcade Publishing • New York

Little, Brown and Company

For my loving and much loved family
— Michael, Rick, Serena, Alexandra, Olivia, and Consuelo

Copyright © 1991 by Pith and Moment Enterprises
All rights reserved. No part of this book may be reproduced in
any form or by any electronic or mechanical means,
including information storage and retrieval systems,
without permission in writing from the publisher,
except by a reviewer who may quote brief passages in a review.

First Edition

Library of Congress Cataloging-in-Publication Data
Going Strong / [interviewed by] Pat York. — 1st ed.
    p.   cm.
    ISBN 1-55970-119-6
    1. Aged — Interviews.   2. Self-realization in old age.   I. York, Pat.
    HQ1061.G64 1991
    305.26 — dc20   91-10704

Published in the United States by Arcade Publishing, Inc., New York,
a Little, Brown company

10 9 8 7 6 5 4 3 2 1
KP
Designed by Robert Reed
Published simultaneously in Canada by Little, Brown & Company
(Canada) Limited
Printed in the United States of America

Contents

Preface

My major inspiration for *Going Strong* was my grandmother. My early impressions were of her protective presence encouraging me, instilling me with confidence, dissipating my despairs, replacing them with laughter and joy, and forcing me to blunder into my own creativity. She was always noticed, not only because she was beautiful and dressed theatrically, but because of the sheer exhilaration that emanated from her. She seemed to know what to leave out and what was essential. She also learned the solutions to life's problems. I took mine to her. She taught me that not everything can be anticipated but that a seeming negative could be changed into a positive.

Because of her influence, her world and mine were infinite and mysterious. I inhaled her warmth, and with it wisdom, and, more often than not, found in my future relationships the qualities she represented. Her support, her humor, and my desire to be physically close to her have instilled in me permanent affection for her generation.

I have always liked people of every age, nationality, and personality. Recently, I realized that most of my photographic and journalistic assignments were not reflecting my diverse interests but were centered around the colorful, yet restricted, entertainment world. An urgency grew within me to relate my work to the world in a different way.

The idea came to me to photograph and interview men and women seventy-five years of age and older. My criteria were that they should have no immediate intention of retiring, they show a great zest for life, and all should make a real contribution to society.

I wanted to produce a work that would be inspirational to all ages: to the old by vivid example of how life can be led to its fullest, to the young by showing the unlimited potential of their own lives. The subjects I sought had chosen to pursue lives in which values of hard work, humor, and tenacity were important. I asked all the participants identical questions:

8

Preface

- What have you learned about yourself?
- Where do you get your creative force and energy?
- What does God mean to you?
- In your life, please describe what you have enjoyed the most, what has pleased you the most, and what has truly made you happy.
- Is there anything that in the past you would not have told anyone, but now in retrospect, you wish you had shown of yourself?
- Do you think it is important to share your life with another human being?
- Do you have a personal formula you have followed?
- Can you sum up — in a few sentences — words to inspire others?
- Are you doing now what you set out in life to do?
- Which of your parents had the more profound influence on you? Was there a precept they imbued in you that you have followed throughout your life?
- What belief has kept you going through hard times?
- Could you describe your working day?
- Do you have a health regime?
- What advice do you have for young people who are embarking on the same career as yours?

I hope that the subjects' varied answers reveal not only their personal philosophies but also the scope of human experience.

Throughout history, and in most cultures, there used to be a traditional reverence for age. This reverence has eroded because of complex reasons, most notably the breakdown of the family unit and the recent overemphasis on the cult of youth. Modern Western society is restless and often tends to ignore the fullness of life. A holistic view encompasses the whole range of age. We are not a sum of compartmentalized parts, each having little relation to the other, but a continuous evolving maturity. Old age is being necessarily redefined, especially as demographics reveal that the population now includes a more mature citizenry. I hope this book mirrors some measure of their prodigious potential.

My practice at the start was to interview a subject first so that the subtle barrier that often exists between a photographer and subject — usually two strangers — could be broken. However, such a system soon proved redundant. As I began interviewing, I found I had immediate empathy with each of the participants. I also had a great deal of fun. I hope this book gives as much pleasure as its participants and production gave to me.

One last note: by the time this book appears, some of its subjects may — by pure actuarial percentages — have passed on to their higher rewards. Indeed, I received Norman Cousins's lively and witty foreword just days before he died. The fact is that he, until the very end, was a living example of what "going strong" means in its purest sense.

— PAT YORK

Foreword

What is perhaps most striking about Pat York's book is that, only a generation ago, it would have been about people over sixty-five who were still in the prime of life and who were active, purposeful, healthy. Today, the fact of a full and rewarding existence after sixty-five is so commonplace that it would seem almost strange that it should command special attention. In the early years of the twenty-first century, there will probably be books about the enjoyment of living after eighty-five.

The worst thing about being seventy-five years old is being treated as a seventy-five-year-old. Being in good health loses some of its charm when people ask about your well-being with the tone of deep concern that makes you wonder whether they know something you don't know. And the joy that comes from hitting a golf ball two hundred yards is somewhat tainted when your younger partner or opponent reacts with admiration born of surprise. Worst of all is getting on the crowded shuttle bus at U.C.L.A. and having several young women spring to their feet and offer their seats.

Spare me your concern and your sympathy. Don't compliment me or whisper to your friend that I still have my marbles if I say something that seems to make sense. Don't stare at my ears as though you wonder whether I have lost my hearing aid without knowing the difference. Don't ask me to show photographs of my great-grandchildren. Don't slap me on the back when you tell a funny story in a way that signals the fact that it's time for me to laugh. Don't assume I am in imminent risk of a hernia if I carry my own bag. Don't turn to each other with knowing looks as though to say that I look pretty good, everything considered. If you are a woman and I compliment you on your appearance, don't react as though I am a dirty old man.

Not so long ago, airline stewardesses would simply hand me a blanket. Now they spread it open and tuck me in. The young lady in the theater box office might at least have the decency to ask me for proof of my age before punching out a reduced-price ticket. Worst of all, perhaps, is that my ten-year-old granddaughter has volunteered the calculation that I have lived more than one-third of the time since the birth of the United States and more than one-half the time since the Civil War.

My wife tells me not to dwell on these things but to concentrate instead on winning both the over-eighty tennis and golf championships as soon as I am eligible. Good advice.

Meanwhile, a friendly plea to people who have something to say to me: Don't shout, just articulate clearly and keep your hands away from your mouth when you speak. And, to the world at large: if I seem to hesitate when I approach a stairway, don't say anything; just

Foreword

point me in the direction of the nearest elevator.

People as a whole have yet to catch up with the fact that the increase in longevity — from forty-four to seventy-four since the turn of the century — has been marked by a corresponding prolongation of good health and intellectual acuity. Research by Dr. George Solomon and his colleagues at U.C.L.A. challenges the prevailing notion that there is an automatic deterioration of the immune system beginning with the age of fifty. Dr. Solomon's research has produced the evidence that people need experience no diminution of their immune function even in advanced age. Systematic testing of a significant number of people beyond the age of seventy-five shows that immune capability resists deterioration so long as reasonably good health is retained. In fact, Dr. Solomon found that the immune systems of fully functional elderly people compare favorably with those of people thirty and forty years younger.

The greatest need of the elderly is to change the attitude of society toward aging. A numbers game dominates public thinking about age. Retirement policies are based on the absurd notion that human capacity falls off significantly at a specified age. Sixty-five was the crucial number until very recently. Sixty-eight or seventy is coming into favor as the critical dividing line. It is undoubtedly true that a decline in various capacities occurs in many people with advancing age, but that decline varies with the individual. It is also true that there can be a falling off with some people at the age of forty or fifty. But the even more significant truth produced by current research is that people can be fully functional ten or fifteen years beyond the customary designated numbers.

No one gets out of this world alive. There is always the statistically certain accident or fatal illness — if one lives long enough. For a nation that needs as many brains and hands as it can apply to its unfinished business, arbitrary standards about aging are not in the national or human interest. We need to develop workable new tests based on functional age rather than chronological absurdities.

No disease in the United States — not cancer, not heart disease, not diabetes, not multiple sclerosis — is more lethal than the boredom that follows retirement. The body goes into a state of rapid deterioration when it loses its reason for being, when mind and muscle are not put to use, and when the individual is surrounded by the perception of society that he or she no longer serves a useful purpose.

Conversely, society needs to recognize that its seasoned people are a continuing and indeed indispensable resource. This acceptance can produce all sorts of wonders. Put it to the test.

The extension of longevity will be the product not just of medical progress but of the changes in the way people think about "old" age. Modern brain research confirms the fact that people tend to move along the path of their expectations. Fears have a way of becoming self-fulfilling. Similarly, reality is fed by recognition of the expanding reach of human consciousness wedded to human aspiration.

The value of Pat York's book is to be found in the demonstrations of purposeful living it provides. She helps us to recognize that it is important to get the most out of whatever is possible.

Here, then, is a guidebook to what is literally the most rewarding experience in the world — the harvest period of one's life in which abilities and relationships can be in full flower.

— NORMAN COUSINS
November 1990

George Abbott

George Abbott was born in Forestville, New York, on June 27, 1887. In 1913, after attending the University of Rochester and Harvard College, Mr. Abbott started his career as an actor. He subsequently became a director and producer. Mr. Abbott's Broadway productions include some of the most celebrated works in American theater: **A Tree Grows in Brooklyn, Boy Meets Girl, Call Me Madam,** *and* **The Boys from Syracuse.** *Mr. Abbott has won four Tony awards and four Donaldson awards, and in 1983 he was honored by the Kennedy Center for the Performing Arts. He is considered to be one of the most eminent Broadway directors/ producers.*

I attribute my longevity to my bloodline. Members of my family have led pretty long lives. I've led a good temperate life and haven't ruined my body much.

Early on in my life, I read the work of Montaigne. His sayings, such as "The value of life lies, not in the length of days, but in the use we make of them; a man may live long, yet live very little. Satisfaction in life depends not on the number of your years, but on your will," greatly influenced my thinking and have helped me through some hard times. I'm also a Darwin man. I think that the world can all be explained by his theory.

Thirty years ago I wrote my autobiography, under my Montaigne influence, in which I told all — bedwetting, getting gonorrhea. The actors, of course, always want to know about me, and every new set of actors I work with comes with my book for me to autograph. I think they must be stealing copies from libraries because they're only in rare-book stores now.

I'm currently working on a musical about Frankenstein. It's a modern melodramatic farce. I've got a new composer, Joseph Turrin, who is very good. Like an opera, "Frankenstein" has arias and songs in it. The book's all done. I'm in rehearsal. We rehearse at night because the York Theater is also a church. I go down there at six P.M. and rehearse until eleven. That's five hours — Equity says that's all the concentration an actor can stand. It is an off-Broadway production.

Generally I get up fairly early. My wife, Joy, is a night owl, so we don't get to sleep until one o'clock or so. Nonetheless, I'm used to getting up at seven A.M. I sit down and write. I do my work in the daytime. In the theater business, where we are making changes all the time, you make them when you have to. And if you're in rehearsal and your scene has to be done by the next day, you work at night so you'll be ready in the morning. I would not say I have any definite work pattern.

I love work, dancing, golf, swimming, and exercising. Work can be terrible when it doesn't come off, but when it does, it's very satisfying. Enjoying play as well as work is very important. I fortunately like healthy food and healthy activities. I like what you're supposed to do — eat, exercise, and not have any addictions. I'm not a workaholic, because I certainly love to

George Abbott

play, but during most of my life I have done two or three shows every year. I've always had something in the fire.

My father was a drinker, so I was brought up to hate liquor. I never drank at all; all through the time that I was going out every night with dancing girls, I never had a drink. But then I came to a point where I thought, "This is bigoted of me; all my friends whom I admire drink, so I'll drink wine when I want to." I started drinking wine with dinner, but I don't much care for it. Whenever I was thinking of smoking, my mother told me, "It can't do you any good, it may do you some harm, and it's expensive." That last reason hit me.

I'm a "now" fellow and a "future" fellow. I have made mistakes that I have regretted, but I never dwell on them. One of my biggest mistakes was marrying Mary Sinclair. Our marriage lasted five years. I had lived with Mary for a year and she'd never shown me one bit of bad temper, yet the day we were married she flew in a great rage at me. I asked her, "How come you never had any of these rages when we lived together?" And she said, "I never had any rights."

I've shared my life now and then with another person in a kind of transitory way. I'm a bit of a loner, but being married to Joy for six years has been a great comfort to me. I've known her for thirty or forty years. When I met her I thought of myself as just a young fellow, but I was seventy years old, she reminded me recently.

My mother was a big influence in my life. (My father was scarcely present. He was a strange man who came around once in a while.) If I have any regrets, it is that I didn't do more for my mother. I gave her a house and a car, all the physical things, but I didn't visit enough. I didn't go to my mother's funeral, if that's important. I was in rehearsal.

If you want to get into the theater, it's a good idea to find out whether or not you have any talent. If you do, get into regional theater. Go where the livin' is easy, where the competition is small, and learn. The only way to get experience is to get experience. If you go around looking for a job in New York, you won't get one until you've proven something. In the old days, we used to go from door to door, from office to office, looking for jobs. Now they have casting agencies who handle everything. The casting people haven't got any real authority. They bring you some awful misfits, but they do give young actors a chance to be seen, where maybe if they went to the door and said, "I've never done anything; would you like to try me out for your show?" they would be turned away.

I thought of grand things when I was in high school, like being a poet. I was a good amateur actor and so I wrote farces to do myself, and that's how I drifted into the theater.

The story of how I got involved with Hal Prince goes back to my ex-wife, Mary Sinclair. She had a group of eager beavers working for her. One especially smart boy was Hal. When Mary's organization failed, I said, "Do you want to work for me?" He stayed on and worked as a gofer, then as assistant stage manager. Then he went to war. I said, "Well, when you come back, I'll give you a job." When he returned the first thing he did was head for my office. I gave him a job. He worked as an assistant stage manager and then he and the stage manager wanted to become producers. Hal and he brought me a show about a pajama factory that I didn't think much of, but they persuaded me to work on it. So they were the producers and I was the director and co-author. That became the immensely successful *Pajama Game.* Hal was always the smart one.

I plan to make Florida my permanent home. Joy and I live on a little crime-free island. Joy loves the garden and has lots of roses and trees.

Going Strong

I like the climate and we've got two neighbors with swimming pools. I've got a lot of projects in mind, one with Charles Strouse, a composer who's working on "Annie II."

Joy feeds me a vitamin and I take something for the bones, too. I fell and broke a hip and an arm. I said to my grandson, "I've been thrown from horses, I played eight years of football, and I never broke a bone." He said, "Grandpa, those weren't the same bones!"

"I love work, dancing, golf, swimming, and exercising."

Alice Acheson

Alice Acheson, wife of former Secretary of State Dean Acheson, was born on August 12, 1895, in Charlevoix, Michigan. Mrs. Acheson attended Wellesley College, the Boston School of Design, and the Corcoran Art School.

Her works have been exhibited in several galleries, including the Corcoran, the Marie Steiner, and the Argent.

M y advice is to work and do what you want to do. I don't really take myself awfully seriously and probably could have more ambition. I paint for the joy of painting, and the financial recompense.

To be a painter and a sculptor, you have to be resolute. I can't emphasize that enough. You must concentrate on exhibiting. It makes a great difference where and how you exhibit. But that is often just chance, and it's hard to do it exactly right. It's wonderful if you have the luck to find a mentor.

Artists are often not as efficient as other people. I think that's a drawback. First of all, to survive you have to be tenacious, healthy, and efficient. You can't do all the things you'd like to do. When I have a firm date for an exhibition, I always work better. I need that goal.

I meant to carry my painting further than I have. I intended to be a portrait painter, but my time was limited, with children and a husband. Landscapes are easier for me and I'm happier doing them.

Although I have a studio, I prefer to paint outdoors. At times, I even paint from my car, which people think is rather astonishing. If you paint outdoors, you have to carry an easel, a stool, an umbrella, and your painting tools; and then if it begins to rain a little bit, you're done for. Remaining inside my car has solved all these problems for me. When I lived in Georgetown, the police would let me park on the side of the street and protect me while I finished my painting.

I think it's essential for a widow not to give up; she must keep on with her own interests.

My mother was both a painter and a musician and I seem to have paid more attention to her than to my father. She didn't go to college; she had been educated at home by a governess. My older sister played the piano and sang. My father was also a musician, so from the time I was ten onward we had family music every night after dinner. People today should realize how fulfilling it is to spend time with their family. Those memories have enriched my life. I took all the art courses they had at Wellesley, which wasn't a great deal. I got married while I was still in college. Then I went to Oxford, and my husband went to law school in Cambridge. We came down to Washington, when he became the secretary to Justice Brandeis on the Supreme Court. Much later on, my husband became President Truman's Secretary of State.

When it comes to my health I try to be sensible. I never smoked and drink very little. I like to swim, dive, canoe, take camping trips, and play tennis. I do walk every day. I take vitamin C. I eat more than you think. I don't seem to put on weight.

Like most people, I try to do the right thing. And I do have a slight feeling that some kind of intelligence knows what you are doing.

Sir (Edwin) Hardy Amies

Sir Hardy, Dressmaker by Appointment to Her Majesty The Queen, was born on July 17, 1909. During the 1930s, he learned his craft at the shops of W. & T. Avery in Birmingham and Lachasse in London. Mr. Amies served in the British Intelligence Corps during World War II, participating in a Special Forces mission to Belgium in 1944. In 1946, he founded and became director of Hardy Amies Ltd.

Mr. Amies has won several prizes, including the **Harper's Bazaar** *award in 1962, the Caswell-Massey award in 1962, 1964, and 1968, and the* **Sunday Times** *special award in 1965.*

Mr. Amies is also the author of several books, including **Just So Far** *(1954),* **ABC of Men's Fashion** *(1964), and* **Still Here** *(1984).*

I am lucky to have enjoyed, for the most part, good health. I've done my best, without making it a fetish to keep it so. In forty years I really have not used any traditional medicine other than homeopathy. What you can't do today, you can always do tomorrow. Just relax about it.

For forty years I have played tennis quite seriously every Saturday and Sunday. I do most of my reading in bed and prefer to limit my social evenings. One of the advantages of being eighty is that you are almost always the oldest in the room and it's easier to leave a party.

I don't understand why the world is what it is. I feel that you must enjoy it. A rose enjoys being a rose; a dog enjoys being a dog. I am content to be Hardy Amies. I would not enjoy myself at anybody else's expense. You've got to fit in and dispense happiness, which is the greatest fulfillment.

Building my business has given me great joy. I am glad that it is still there and that I am still its sole owner. I never had the slightest idea that I would be knighted. When the letter came, I was alone, and I just sat down and burst into tears. It's a personal gift. Other people who get it are much more important than just a dressmaker. The senior one of us, Norman Hartnell, set the pattern. He had done much more for the Queen than I have because he started to dress her when she was quite young. And, also, he did a lot for the Queen Mother, for whom I have never made anything. I am proud that for many years we have had a haute couture business, and I am equally pleased we now also enjoy royalties around the world for quite a substantial sum for licensee operations.

In September we are invited to Japan to celebrate our twentieth anniversary working there. To the Japanese we represent the spirit of England. While it may seem pompous, I have enjoyed playing this English role. Through my work, I've been able to play this role all over the world. I've traveled extensively to Australia, New Zealand, India, and America. For the past twenty years, I've greatly en-

Sir (Edwin) Hardy Amies

joyed keeping an apartment in New York.

Recently Hardy Amies Ltd. established offices in Taiwan and Korea. For twenty to thirty years we have been designing for men. We thump the drum for the English style, which has become universal. With women it's more difficult to define the English style. An understated look of clothes is associated with this country. All the British upper classes look like they have come up from the country to London. We are not an urban race; we are a country race that goes to London for fun.

I don't think it is important to share your life with one person, but to have a lot of friends makes all the difference in the quality of your life. I have always loved houses and having dinner parties and running them well. I admire very much the American author Edith Wharton, who prized order. Making a house and garden in the country has brought me great enjoyment. My house, previously a schoolhouse, was a shell to which I added rooms.

I started the dress designing business after having observed and been inspired by my mother's work as a court dressmaker. She really understood her customers and had an excellent sense of style. Her adult friends as well as mine all worked in the business and I grew up listening to their chatter. At twenty-four, I was offered a manager's job in an existing fashion store. I had no practical experience but I did understand the intricacies of that field. I learned designing by watching and talking to the customers. A well-heeled family took me under their wing. From them I learned about the lives of the English upper class and chose that segment of society to be my clientele.

I am proud that Ken Fleetwood, who has worked with me for thirty-odd years, has been accepted by the Queen. They obviously get on well, because the Queen orders handsomely through him.

I was very lucky that my father sent me for three and a half years to France and Germany immediately after I left school. Knowing both languages has been a tremendous help in my life.

I suppose you could call me an optimist; I have always had a sense that adversity would pass. When I was sixty-three, I sold the business. Seven years later, the company who had acquired mine ran into problems. So, at the age of seventy, I bought the business back. It was a big risk, but I am pleased I did it.

My working week in London is from Tuesday to Friday mornings only. I have breakfast in bed at seven forty-five: grapefruit juice, weak tea, lemon with one sugar, two pieces of toast made by my cook in the country with a quantity of corn roughage, and marmalade with an orange and apple. My chauffeur picks me up at eight A.M.

Ken Fleetwood, my right hand in the company and second in command in the business, and I arrive at our showroom at half past nine. If I am going to dinner, I keep my lunch very light. In the evening, if I am home, I'll just have a bowl of soup. I love the theater and go to all the major opera performances. Friday mornings I go to the country.

I have never had a headache.

My advice for future dress designers is first to decide who they want to design for. It's important to target specifically. No designer can create for everybody.

The top dress designers are "bespoke" dressmakers. This is an English word. It is what the French call *haute couture:* ordering clothes especially for you and having them custom-made. The reason my business is still reasonably successful rests on the fact that I have always had a team of first-class fitters and tailors. This wonderful team has kept the business going.

I have had no secrets.

Going Strong

In earlier years a man who didn't marry was not as accepted as he is today, but today, provided you lead a reasonably respectable life, nobody gives a damn. I know there is a whole race of men who have no desire to go to bed with women and procreate children. I think that perhaps it's nature telling us there are too many people in the world. I have never really been unhappy about that. I have had a lot of fun and at eighty I am still interested in these matters.

My advice about retirement is, if you are still interested in your work, keep working. You should only retire if you are going to be happier, because your work has become monotonous and irksome. If you do retire, take up gardening or orchid growing or something you can become passionate about.

"Each age has an order and can be enjoyed to the hilt."

Tom Angove

Tom Angove, the maintenance manager for the Minack Theater, was born in 1914. He helped to build the open-air Minack Theater in Cornwall, England. What is remarkable is that he, with the idea's founder, Rowena Cade, built the entire structure by hand, hewing the rocks and collecting the raw materials from around the area. The theater has flourished since its opening. Mr. Angove works there every day of the week, ensuring that everything is in order for the year-round season.

My hair is turning white but my spirit is unchanged. There's no such thing as old age if you don't think about it. Early retirement or any retirement is not for me. My energy and my health come from working.

I get up at half past seven and I come to the theater at eight o'clock and I'm here until four o'clock. If there's any repairing to do, I'll do it, and then I go home. I've worked here since 1953. You've got to work. I don't get one day off — work seven days a week — that's what I like.

What I've enjoyed the most is working in this theater. I met Rowena Cade when I was six years old. She was a wonderful woman. I remember that she had a car, an old Bullnose Morris, and she used to take us for rides — it was lovely, and she was so kind to me. I came to work with her in 1953 and I helped her build the Minack open-air theater here near Land's End. She started the theater in the winter of 1931 and I became the builder's mate in 1953. It's been going since then, except for the war years. She started it up right after the war. I was so proud to work on it and for her.

I was working on a farm, and then in a mill, and then I was thirty-six and a half years working in the auxiliary coast guard. I was presented with a medal by Prince Charles. I did all these jobs at the same time. The farm was small — only sixteen acres. I had cattle, and also I used to grow early potatoes and early flowers. I gave the farm up in 1972.

I don't take vitamins, but I eat a lot of vegetables. Being in the open and working keeps you healthy.

I was one of ten children, and six of my brothers and sisters were away in the Second World War and that was quite a time for my mother. I've got a wife and daughter, and they've brought me a lot of pleasure. If you get on with people, it makes life a lot better.

Dame Peggy Ashcroft

The world-famous, Oscar-winning British actress Dame Peggy Ashcroft was born on December 22, 1907. She began her career with the Birmingham Repertory Theater in 1926. In the early 1930s, she moved to the London stage, where she played her first Shakespearean roles at the Old Vic Theater. In 1968, she became a director of the Royal Shakespeare Company.

Dame Peggy made her film debut in 1933. Her films include **The Wandering Jew, The Thirty-nine Steps,** *and* **The Nun's Story.** *In 1985, Dame Peggy won an Academy Award for her role in* **A Passage to India** *(1984). In 1984 she won the BAFTA Award for the television series* **The Jewel in the Crown.**

What I think matters most is family, friends, and work — in that order.

Brooke Astor

The foundation executive and philanthropist Brooke Astor was born in 1903 in Portsmouth, New Hampshire. She has been a consulting editor at **House and Garden** *magazine since 1946. Mrs. Astor is president and trustee of the Vincent Astor Foundation and is a corporate board member of the Astor Home for Children. She also is a Lifetime Trustee of Rockefeller University. In 1988, President Reagan awarded her the Presidential Citizen's Medal and that same year she also received the National Medal of the Arts from the National Endowment for the Arts.*

Mrs. Astor has written several books, including **Patchwork Child** *(1962),* **The Bluebird Is at Home** *(1965),* **Footprints** *(1980), and* **The Last Blossom on the Plum Tree** *(1986).*

I am told that I must be quite a strong person to have become as old as I am. Discipline is very important, in every way — in my mind, my body. I can't ever be too disciplined in my work because, since I love people and I love to communicate, that can be a distraction.

My working day starts a little after eight A.M. and goes on uninterruptedly from morning 'til night. Twice a week I do yoga. Then I'm on the go. I do an enormous amount of telephoning. I go to the office. I'm on all these boards. Today, for example, I gave a lunch for forty-five people to endow a curatorship. At two-thirty P.M. I'm off to the library or back to the office. I don't walk as much as I like to in New York. It's dangerous now, not fun. I go out every single night. I don't belong to a clique. I see young people, old people, people from different economic levels. I've got all sorts of friends — to me what's most important is that they be fun and stimulating. I prefer to be with people who know more than I do. I walk three or four miles every day, swim every weekend, and get a great deal of outdoor exercise. And I always like to watch the sunsets

on the Hudson River. It's a kind of religion for me.

I take aspirin, iron, and calcium. I've never had a face-lift. I'm not going to. But I had my neck done, years ago, when I was about forty. I have a lot of energy. And I'm not introspective. I feel as though I am an untouchable now. I don't feel, and never did feel, jealousy or envy.

I went to the best school in Washington, Miss Madeira's School, as well as to the best dancing class. When I was young, I never knew if I was rich or poor. It was considered bad form to talk about money. I never thought whether the other girls had big houses or more things. Everybody came back to my house and I went to theirs. I was perfectly happy. I was an only child with much love. I had a marvelous childhood.

My mother said, "Don't die guessing." Keep your intellectual curiosity going. Don't ever stop. Don't ever stop reading. Reading is a way of life. I've never been so unhappy that nature and reading haven't helped me. Mother started reading Walter Scott to me when I was

Brooke Astor

five. Then I took to writing plays myself, and keeping diaries. We lived in China for four years, from the time I was seven to eleven. Father told me I could have anything I like if I learned Chinese, which I did, of course. It was mere coolie talk, but I did enjoy it.

Reading and men have been a very enjoyable part of my life. I like attention from men. I was brought up to flirt and that's gone out of style now. It's a pity. Girls today take life too seriously. They have these love affairs, but it's all so serious.

I had a miserable first marriage. Looking back now, I wonder how I lived through it, but I did. I used to cry, I was so miserable. I was just seventeen when I married and I was still curtseying to people. I didn't notice that my husband was a drunkard. His family was very rich. My mother was against the marriage. It started because a friend of mine got mumps and couldn't go to the Princeton prom at the last moment. They couldn't get anybody else except me. This student treated me like a grown-up and took me seriously. He began sending me poetry books. My mother was roaring with laughter saying, "What is this? How perfectly absurd!" And the family came down in their private car. Everybody thought this is a wonderful marriage. I didn't realize his family was hoping to get somebody to marry him. Well, I couldn't control him. They had brought him up very badly, he'd never been to boarding school and when he went to Princeton they sent him with two French mechanics, two racing cars, and twenty-five thousand dollars spending money (which in those days was quite a lot).

While I didn't have specific goals in life, I think somebody has guided me in some way and I haven't made a mess of it, though I might have, being rather gullible and trusting. When I was pregnant, my first husband got drunk and hit me on the jaw and broke it. For that

sort of thing today people would go to psychiatrists or even prison, in some cases. I don't remember being unhappy. My father said, "You must leave him, leave him at once." And I said, "No, I've got to have the baby. I'm not going to leave him when he's fathered my child." I stayed on and he drank like a fish and finally he got tired of me. And left me. I never would have left him. I felt like laying a carpet out in front of the woman who took him away from me, I was so glad. She was ten years older and knew much more.

My second husband dropped dead in front of me. He was the love of my life, and I was married to him for twenty years, and it was marvelous. We lived in Portofino. We loved to walk with rucksacks on our backs and we loved to dance. I had a wonderful life. When he died, I thought I would die; I could not live without him.

Eleven months later, I married Vincent, his brother-in-law. He was miserable and unhappy. He persuaded me to marry him and finally I said yes. Vincent owned *Newsweek* and the St. Regis Hotel. We never went anywhere. He never wanted to go out at all. I took music lessons every day and I sang, played the piano, played backgammon. I loved him because he was lonely and he had never known love. He had a miserable childhood and was married twice before me. I don't think he was happy in either of those marriages. He never really knew what it was like to have any real home life. I don't suppose we went out seven times in seven years. We lived in a house in Maine, and had a marvelous life. Then he died, in 1959. I've had chances to marry again, but I never will. I do get a little bit lonely, which I never used to. I'd have to marry somebody the proper age, I couldn't marry a much younger man, that would look out of place.

Vincent talked to me a lot about the foundation because he was leaving it to me. He said,

Going Strong

"You're going to have a marvelous time with this when I'm gone." Well, I have. He was very suspicious of people, and I didn't realize he was going to leave me the foundation to do absolutely what I liked with it. It's been a crusade on my part. Fortunately, I've had for the past twelve years a marvelous directress, Linda Gillis, who likes what I like. I never give to anything I don't see.

This money was made by John Jacob Astor. When he came to this country in 1783 he was a German peasant with a pound in his pocket. It was given to him by his brother, who had gone to England and had started a music shop. He brought over six violins, one pound, and two suits, and he started here, in New York, and he ended up in 1846 dying the richest man in America — twenty million dollars. Which is nothing today. But in those days the second richest man was a member of the Goelet family and he only had two million. He was supposed to have made his money in furs, but he made most of his money in real estate. So I thought I'd give it back to New York.

When I inherited the foundation, I went to John Rockefeller (the oldest of the Rockefeller brothers) and I really didn't know him well at all. I called him up and said, "Mr. Rockefeller, may I come and see you and ask your advice?" He said, "Just come and lunch with me." I went, and he said that the most important thing is that the person who has the money should know where it is going. If you have the money, you should be really interested in it and not leave it to someone else. You've got to be involved, you've got to care about it. And I've turned down things that I'm not going to be interested in. We must get a couple of thousand applications a year and we sit there and we go through them. We gave two million dollars to help for the renovation of Carnegie Hall, a marvelous old hall. The acoustics are sublime. You can't have a foundation unless you really care. We never give to individuals. You have to make certain rules. You can't be all over the place.

The old Bible says it's more blessed to give than to receive. And in giving you do receive, an enormous amount, back. If I go to a hospice and see people, it makes a lot of difference to them. Whereas if I was just sitting in an office writing out checks, the way most people do who are philanthropists, it would not mean so much. I have given up my life to it, I really have. I might have gotten married again. But I never could marry and give up the name of Astor because it is so linked with the foundation. Also I couldn't have given the time. If I wanted to have a happy marriage, I couldn't have done what I'm doing now. Any man worth his salt wouldn't put up with it. Because I do work very hard. But it isn't work. I love it. I feel very grateful that I've had this chance.

Irina Baronova-Tennant

Irina Baronova was born in St. Petersburg, Russia, in 1916. In 1920, her family escaped the Bolshevik Revolution by going to Romania. Eight years later, they moved to France.

Baronova began dancing professionally with the Paris Opéra. In 1932, she became a soloist in a George Balanchine production of **Orpheus in the Underworld** *and then joined the Ballets Russes de Monte Carlo.*

She is a Fellow of the Royal Academy of Dancing in London, where she has been an instructor for master classes in dancing and mime.

I play life by ear. Whichever way it goes, it's much more fun that way. Otherwise life becomes too regimented and you don't see sideways. I'd need about three lifetimes to do what I'd like to do, the time goes so quickly.

Every day after lunch, from two to six, I go to my room with my typewriter and reference files and I work on my book of memoirs. There are some topics that I wouldn't talk about before for private reasons, but now I am an old lady and it doesn't matter.

I've been coaching ballet all over the world. Two years ago, I was in Australia with the Australian National Ballet giving classes, coaching and restaging *Les Sylphides* for them. I have been asked to be one of the judges for the New York International Ballet Competition. I give lectures in England, France, and America on our dance techniques and about the people I've worked with.

I was very lucky in the days of the Ballets Russes. I worked with Chagall and [Alexander] Benois, who was a very old man then, but he

Irina Baronova-Tennant

was marvelous. Those wonderful composers, like Rachmaninoff and Stravinsky, would come and play at our rehearsals and would attend every costume fitting and even discuss the colors and shapes of various costumes. The Ballets Russes were also very lucky in having the greatest choreographers, such as the old Fokine, Nijinsky, and Balanchine. We worked with all of them, the best of our country, all at the same time.

I have learned two things in life: the first is not to be self-centered, because there are too many people around you who are worth listening to and observing. It's best to try to understand someone's point of view even if you don't agree with it. Second, never lose your sense of humor. Whatever happens, try to giggle about it and it will seem less important. This is easier said than done, but worth trying.

Life teaches you. If you stop to think about things you've done in the past, you often see, in hindsight, how you might have done them better. I think that with age, you become more aware and put more thought into a project. When you're young you are often spontaneous, and a bit arrogant. Sometimes I wish I could turn the clock back in time.

Most young people love to dance, but they don't realize how much mental and physical discipline is required. Like any athlete, a dancer can never give up daily work and exercise. There are no holidays for dancers. You may get three weeks of "official" holiday a year, but your muscles immediately become flabby without daily class. As a young dancer you must realize that you have to give up a lot of your private life without resentment, because there is something else you like better — the profession you chose. The work is very hard and it must be accomplished with intelligence. There is much more to being a good dancer than just standing at the bar and doing

your exercises. As a future dancer it is important to learn the history of the theater, music, the history of costume, so that you arrive fully equipped to take on any role. A dancer might think that you can walk out on stage the same way in *Swan Lake* as you would in *Sleeping Beauty*, but you really can't. If you know the story behind the ballet, you'll know that the two ballets are quite different in style. Unless you do your homework, you will never achieve artistic professionalism.

Ballet requires more rigor and discipline than any other dance form. When you dance you've got to sing the music inside, so your movements express and explain what you are trying to say. An actor has got a voice and words from a script. For dancers, every gesture we make expresses either the story or the emotions of our ballet.

My first success as a dancer, which was very early on, encouraged me and really made me love what I was doing. The other most wonderful event in my life was the birth of each of my children. I don't think any other experience can top that miracle.

I still miss my father enormously. He dropped dead of a heart attack at the age of fifty-seven. He taught me to appreciate art. On Sundays when we lived in Paris, we would always go to the museums, or take walks through the streets by the Seine. He would show and explain things to me, in such a way that it was like a magical fairy tale. He loved music and played the violin and the cello. I learned to play piano, and we used to play together. I always preferred spending my free days with my father, because it was much more fun than seeing people my own age. It's so important to give your children and grandchildren inspiration like what he gave me. Teach them to notice, to pay attention, to appreciate and to be inquisitive. Don't just look,

Going Strong

try to see. My father kindled a sort of curiosity in me that I have kept, and it makes life much more full to this day.

After my husband was killed in a car accident, I had no choice but to keep myself together. The kids were young and I had no right to fall apart; they needed me. And their need gave me the strength to keep going.

"Never lose your sense of humor."

The Reverend H. J. C. Bowden

The Reverend Henry James Charles Bowden, an Episcopal priest, was born in Bushwick, Georgia, in 1901. Father Bowden attended Morehouse College and has been a priest since his graduation. He now works primarily with the elderly in such organizations as the Fulton County Council on Aging, in addition to conducting some church services.

I was born and reared in a seacoast town in southeast Georgia. Race relations there when I was a boy were fairly good, but in other parts of the state they were not. I've always had certain standards regardless of prevailing customs. For example, I will never accept, because I am black, the fact that someone who is another complexion should have rights over me. Know who you are and be proud of it.

I am constantly trying to be of service to humanity, and this pursuit has kept me going. When I came into the ministry, the Depression was upon us. I had a growing family and didn't appreciate the importance of the struggles at the time, but, in retrospect I know the Depression made me and others stronger.

For three years I served a parish in Wilmington, North Carolina, during the worst part of the Depression. Sometimes the sacrifices we were called on to make were not appreciated. It was hurtful to hear some members of the congregation say, "We can't jeopardize what our forebears have done in order to support a stranger." My message was to share the burden and rise above the panic and crisis.

I haven't allowed the many setbacks to deter me from trying to follow the path that I obligated myself to follow. I've never become so disillusioned that I've wanted to throw up my hands. Fortunately, my wife has always been very supportive. We met at Morehouse College, where we were both students.

I have been most blessed and have had very few illnesses. However, when I wanted a commission (in the military), I was told, "You've been digging your grave with your teeth." I weighed two hundred eighteen pounds. I had big jaws. I thought I was in the pink of health, but I wasn't acceptable, and it floored me. My brother, a physician, advised me to lose weight and I have been weight-conscious and healthy ever since.

I've been a minister since 1928 and was fortunate to begin my ministry working for a very large Episcopal parish in New York City. I was called a junior curate. After a while, I wanted a different situation and moved to San Antonio, Texas, where I lived for two years.

I must have been five or six years old when I knew I wanted to be a priest in the Episcopal church. My home was a block from the church my family attended. My parents' devotion to religion has greatly influenced my decisions.

I am identified with the Fulton County Council on Aging, an advocacy organization designated under the Old Americans Act. I have not retired from the church, but officially have no duties. But I still often perform volunteer services in the Saint Paul's Episcopal Church.

Throughout my life I have tried to make positive contributions to my heritage. I've worked towards freedom and fairness for all humans regardless of the color of their skin. And I believe that the future holds a lot for us if we work together as loving human beings.

George Burns

The world-famous Oscar-winning actor, comedian, radio and television pioneer George Burns was born on January 20, 1896, in New York City. He began his show business career as a child vaudeville performer. In 1926, he married his partner, Gracie Allen. Together, the couple toured the world as "George and Gracie," making their radio debut on the BBC in 1932. Their radio comedy show ran until 1950, at which point the couple successfully turned their talents to television.

Mr. Burns has made over twenty films, winning the Best Supporting Actor award for his role in **The Sunshine Boys** *in 1975 and also starring in the 1977 movie* **Oh, God!** *An accomplished author, Mr. Burns has written* **How to Live to Be 100 or More** *(with David Fisher, 1983),* **Gracie: A Love Story** *(1988), and* **All My Best Friends** *(1989).*

I came from a very big family, seven sisters and five brothers. Very poor. I think we ate one of the sisters. Not true. If we did, we'd have to use ketchup. My mother had a very good sense of humor. My parents had nothing to do with my career; that just happened. I used to feed kids on the East Side. We used to make syrup for a candy store down in the base- ment, and there was a letter carrier, Ollie. He loved harmony singing and he came down the basement once and saw four kids and started teaching us how to sing harmony. We weren't good, but we sang, and then, one day, we looked upstairs (because this was down in the cellar), and there were eight or nine people standing there. They threw some pennies at

36

George Burns

us, so I said, "Fellas, let's get out of the chocolate business and get into show business." We sang in yards, on ferryboats, and on street corners, and we passed around our hats. Sometimes they'd put a penny in our hats and sometimes they took our hats. We lost a lot of hats but we stayed in show business.

I just love what I am doing. I love show business — working in front of an audience. If the audience wasn't good, I couldn't do it. To walk out on the stage and have the audience like you and feel their love come over the footlights helps and motivates me each time. If you asked me to stand up now for an hour, I couldn't, but on the stage I could. The audience gives you that vitality. If people can fall in love with what they do for a living, they'll be around for a long time. There are a lot of people who have to get up in the morning and work all day and don't like what they are doing, but they've got to make a living. I would rather be a failure in something I love than be successful in something I hate. It's nice to be my age, ninety-three, and get out of bed and do something that I'm going to love to do that day. Because at my age I can't make any money in bed.

My life is full. My marriage to Gracie was wonderful. I think marriage is not what you do in bed. A good marriage is when you get out of bed. I was never a great lover. I made Gracie laugh. After you're married twenty-five years and you get in bed with your wife, it's easy to make her laugh.

One night I had too much to drink and I did something with a girl a married man shouldn't do. Over the phone I told Jack Benny I had been silly and what I had done and how sorry I was. The maid came to me and said, "Mr. Burns, Mrs. Burns heard the conversation with Jack Benny over the phone!" Before this episode, Gracie had wanted a seven-hundred-dollar silver centerpiece. I'd told her we had enough silver. After talking to the maid, I went out and bought Gracie a centerpiece and a ten-thousand-dollar diamond ring. She never said a word. Seven years later she said to Mary Benny, "I wish George would cheat again. I need another centerpiece."

She was smart, that Gracie was. It meant nothing, but it could have broken up a wonderful marriage. Everybody thought Gracie was dumb on the stage, but Gracie didn't think so. Gracie thought she was smart on the stage. When Gracie said these strange things and you didn't understand her, she felt sorry for you. Gracie didn't tell a joke, she explained it to you. I shared a wonderful life with Gracie and now I share my life with everybody.

Since I was eight I've been in show business. At first, I wasn't doing well. I did bad acts but I didn't mind; I loved what I was doing. I thought the audiences were bad, not me. At twenty-seven I met Gracie and things turned around and we were a good act. When we first did the acts, I had the jokes and Gracie was the straight woman. Nobody laughed. I noticed that the audience loved Gracie, so I wrote the jokes. What made us a good combination was that I was able to write the jokes and Gracie was able to do them. If I wrote something sarcastic, the audience wouldn't accept that from Gracie. When I went on the stage, I always had to find out first what way the wind was blowing, because if my cigar smoke went into Gracie's face, the audience would hate me.

The only hard time I had was when Gracie passed away. What do you do when people die? There's nothing you can do about that. You cry and you cry and you cry and you finally stop crying. I kept working. I was very lucky that I had something to do because when Gracie passed away, it was terrible.

Going Strong

I don't do anything on the stage that doesn't fit my age. When you are ninety-three and you dress appropriately, it is OK. If you dressed young, you would look a hundred and five.

If I retired, I wouldn't enjoy anything. To wake up in the morning and have nothing to do but play golf or bridge would not be enjoyable. To work and then have a couple of hours free to play golf or bridge is a pleasure. If I retired, I would be waiting to die. My motto is "Don't die. It's been done!"

"Don't die. It's been done!"

John Cage

John Cage was born on September 5, 1912, in Los Angeles. As a student at Pomona College, he studied composition with Arnold Schoenberg and Henry Cowell. In 1944 he became the musical director for the Merce Cunningham Dance Company, a position he has held ever since. Mr. Cage also taught composition at the New School for Social Research in New York City from 1955 to 1960. His many works include "Son of Tree," "Fontana Mix," and "The Freeman Etudes."

In addition to receiving the Ordre des Arts et Lettres from the French Ministère de Culture and participating in the Norton Lecture series at Harvard, Mr. Cage has written several books, including **The Mushroom Book** *(1972),* **M** *(1972), and* **Writings Through Finnegans Wake.**

The thing to do is to become attentive to the world outside you. And then make that interest grow larger rather than smaller. It might well include, as it did for Andy Warhol, the soup cans.

I wanted to retire to Bolivia because they have no interest in modern music. But instead I live in New York now in this loft with Merce Cunningham. When I first walked into this loft and saw how bright it was, I was pleased. We moved right in. When I opened the window and looked downstairs, there was Bolivia!

In my life, I never wanted to find out too much about anything. It's more amusing and makes life more interesting to remain on this side of mystery, rather than the side of knowing.

When Marcel Duchamp was asked about God, he said, "Let's not talk about Him, He's man's stupidest idea." It's an invention on the part of human beings to keep other human beings in line. It's the supreme authority. They said on the radio the other day, on Saint Patrick's Day, they were worried about whether it was going to rain or not for the Saint Patrick's Day Parade. And the Irish people were worried it would rain, so they appealed to the archbishop, and he appealed to his higher authority but it *still* rained. No, I think God is the way human beings have of pushing things aside and putting them in other hands than their own. I'm not speaking against what you might call "the enjoyment of life," or "gratitude for being alive" or a sense of spiritual feelings. But my path is the path of Zen Buddhism, which doesn't bother with God. There's a lovely statement where one of the teachers holds a cat with one hand and a knife in the other and says to his students, "Quick, a word of truth or I slit the cat's throat." Zen itself began with complete silence on the part of Buddha. He went in front of a group and remained silent. He was simply holding a flower. And finally one of the disciples smiled and the Buddha stepped down.

My father was an inventor. As a composer, I enjoyed making some kind of discovery. People speak of the avant-garde, but they

might as well speak of pioneering, or simply discovery. Doing something for the first time is very pleasing to me.

You can't share work with somebody else, and since most of my life is spent working, I have remained somewhat of a hermit. I collaborate with other artists. Merce Cunningham and I live here together. We don't share our lives; he is going about his life and I am going about mine. He needs a dance studio, and since I compose for his dance company, I need to be here. I feel rather like Thoreau. I am better off alone. If there's somebody else around, it spoils the situation. I don't mean that I don't respond to other people particularly, but I don't think that one's work necessarily brings you closer to others.

In the thirties, I devoted my life to music. And now I not only compose music, I also write books. People are curious about my music. And I have grown interested in writing in the same way that I am interested in composing. I have been doing graphic work such as etchings and drawings as well as watercolors. My life's focus and interest constantly change. In the fifties, when I moved to the country, I became a hunter of wild mushrooms, and since living here in New York City, I have become an indoor gardener.

In terms of food, I follow a macrobiotic diet in my own way. I have given up alcohol and caffeine and use spring water for cooking. It is gratifying to know that I did drink at one time and that I was able to give it up and not have any regrets.

I met a marvelous doctor in Germany. Holistic medicine in Germany is more advanced than in other countries. Nothing that the American Medical Association does is helpful. All they do is send you to specialists who know nothing about you as a person. Huge medical bills arrive and no help. I got closely involved with holistic medicine in Frankfurt when I was working on two of my operas. Probably because of the strain of the situation, I suffered a stroke. I felt as if I had been bitten by a spider. I lost all my strength in my left leg, which felt like a piece of spaghetti. It happened on a Friday and I didn't see a doctor until Monday. I did manage to get around. This holistic German doctor cured me in two weeks by means of the bark from a Chinese tree, the ginkgo. He subsequently became my principal doctor.

My day begins after breakfast with the watering of the plants. Days are divided between little watering and big watering. I don't speak to them; I'm the author of silence. Silence speaks louder than words. My music is like the traffic on Sixth Avenue, so they hear that. Then the mail comes. And the telephone rings. As for the telephone, it never ends. What I call my work gets put in between those commitments. Right now I am preparing a new piece for a festival in Switzerland. It's called "Fourteen." It's for one piano and thirteen instruments. Then when I finish the operas I'll go back to the Freeman Etudes which I have been working on. They're very difficult pieces to write. My copyist just has had one since last August, and hasn't finished copying it yet.

I still have a good deal of energy. I've asked Andrew Culpin, who helps me with the construction aspects of my graphic art as well as computer programming, to work with me on one of my new graphic ideas. I give him my concept, and then he arranges the computer program or puts together the objects. And right now he is working on a program whereby I'll be able to make a single stroke with a group anywhere between three and seventeen pencils of varying intensities. The pencils will go in indeterminate directions so that I won't be making an intentional drawing. It will be like a cloud that passes over the paper.

Going Strong

In the early forties, I was married, and my wife, Sandy, and I lived here in New York, totally penniless. One of our friends, John Steinbeck, invited us to the 21 Club for lunch. I remember being so shocked because the lunch cost a hundred dollars. How foolish, we thought, when we needed so much and never knew where the next dinner was coming from.

My advice to a young musician: look over the whole history of music and find out which part interests you the most and then pay attention to it in detail.

"I feel rather like Thoreau. I am better off working alone."

Dr. William G. Cahan

Dr. William G. Cahan, a surgeon, was born in New York City on August 2, 1914. He earned his undergraduate degree from Harvard College and was awarded his medical degree by Columbia University. For forty years, Dr. Cahan was an eminent surgeon at Sloan-Kettering Hospital in New York City. He is now the senior attending surgeon in the Breast Service Center, Memorial Hospital, New York. Dr. Cahan is also an active participant in the campaign against smoking.

*B*eing in good physical shape keeps me going strong. I walk as much as I possibly can and I play singles in tennis at least twice a week with a pro. No smoking, little alcohol, little sleep, moderation in eating and in activities are all parts of my "engine room," which, except for an occasional minor setback, apparently is in good working condition.

Life is so fascinating, I still feel that I'm in its mainstream. . . . My profession continues to motivate me (except for my four hours' sleep) night and day. I enjoy my wonderful wife, children, and grandchildren, but more than that, the sense of having certain "unanswered prayers"; my continuing research toward a cure for cancer, the defeat of tobacco interests, and, of course, the desire to stick around and see my wife Grace's magazine, *Mirabella*, evolve, and, not least, to see if the New York Mets win the pennant.

Whenever my circulation appears to be sluggish, I remind myself of all those who are still smoking and I'm sure corpuscles race fiercely through my vessels.

Both my parents were vigorous people; my father was a fine artist, my mother an interior decorator as well as a crusader for a variety of causes. I function the way mountaineers describe the reason they climb Mount Everest, "because it's there." As long as I am challenged by a cause or an idea, I am able to summon forth energies and, if necessary, battle with it.

My ethic is to be compassionate.

Fortunately, I have been very lucky. Good has far outweighed the bad luck in my life. There are a myriad of things I've enjoyed immensely, particularly some occasional medical miracles. For instance, there has been many a time when other physicians had given up on a patient whose advanced cancer was considered inoperable. Soon after coming to me and undergoing treatment, the patient survived. Those medical and human victories have made my life as a cancer specialist profoundly worthwhile.

Since 1950, when a connection between smoking and lung cancer first became evident, I have been on the barricades of the antitobacco movement and tried to help abolish what has been called "one of the most grievous examples of destructive behavior in the history of mankind."

One in every three adult patients at Memorial Hospital would not be there had they not smoked. Over thirty thousand papers have been written on the hazards of tobacco, yet the tobacco companies and their executives still have the nerve to claim that it is harmless and just a mere habit. Fifty-five million Americans continue to smoke, most of whom wish they

Dr. William G. Cahan

could stop but can't because they are totally addicted. Smoking is not just a habit; it is an addiction which proves more difficult to shake than cocaine, heroin, or alcoholism.

I only sleep a little and have always done so. At two A.M. I wake up after four hours of sleep. This leaves me four hours of peace and quiet during which I feel at my sharpest. It is in those early hours that I do most of my writing. Having finished all that I have to write, I may turn on the TV and catch the latest news. By then it is seven A.M. and Grace wakes up. We have breakfast together.

Two months ago, I decided to stop practicing surgery and became emeritus at Memorial Sloan-Kettering Cancer Center.

Although I feel totally equipped and psychologically and physiologically able to continue, I thought it best and graceful to stop at this time and open the path to a younger surgeon.

Hospital laws dictate that you have to retire at the age of seventy. Originally, the age for retirement was sixty-five, but then New York State changed its laws, and retirement age was extended to seventy. Nevertheless, it still seemed unjust and irritating to retire someone purely on the basis of a chronologic age. I fought this law. Upon learning of my impending retirement, my patients were so disturbed that they wrote letters and made calls to the hospital's executives. There was even a group of them threatening to picket the hospital. I was eventually permitted to see patients in follow-up but could no longer perform surgery.

Subsequently, New York State passed yet another new law forbidding mandatory retirement on the basis of age alone, and I was able to resume surgery.

I have been at Memorial Hospital since January of 1942, except for three years in the Air Force during World War II. Grateful patients of mine, along with some good friends, have donated over eight million dollars to the hospital for buildings, laboratories, and research.

I was never more touched than on my seventy-fifth birthday, when I received, as a gift from my wife, a breast cancer research laboratory named after me and endowed by her as well as a conference room from Ann and Herb Siegel.

As a physician, I am not alone in being disturbed about the way medicine seems to be heading. The deterioration in the patient-physician relationship distresses me.

There are far too many uncaring physicians who seem to present a chromium-plated facade and do not follow patients postoperatively or who will not take the time to discuss their condition with them. Understanding the nature of one's condition is essential for a patient. I particularly resent those physicians who do not return patients' phone calls. If our medical profession is to survive, then we doctors must be less like plumbers and more like artists.

For the patients who have been callously treated, I advise them to drop their physician and seek another one with whom they can have a total rapport. There are times when a life-and-death decision needs to be made, and you must be comfortable with your doctor in those dramatic moments.

A personal crisis probably played a major role in influencing me in becoming a physician.

My grandmother had a heart attack and died in my arms. I was fourteen at the time and I vowed then that I would never be in such a helpless position again.

People often ask how I can "stand it." What I am able to do is transfer my concern for their cancer into instantly thinking of ways to correct it.

Going Strong

Cancer is a difficult adversary; to use an often cited metaphor, it is the enemy. Because it begins so insidiously, it is often well advanced when it is detected. Once a patient is in my charge, I try everything in my power to overcome their cancer. I suppose this reflects in the way I play tennis to some degree. I do run for every drop shot and every lob as if my life depended on it . . . as if it were a championship. In cancer research, always trying the utmost — but knowing when to stop — is a virtue.

Practicing prevention remains the best way to practice medicine.

Although I no longer perform surgery (my lung cancer operating room was called "Marlboro Country"), I remain nonetheless deeply active in my antitobacco activities. The writing of my autobiography as well as my involvement in my wife's magazine, *Mirabella,* occupy the rest of my time.

My best advice for a successful life is to continue to work with all the means at one's disposal as long as health permits.

"If our medical profession is to survive, then we doctors must be less like plumbers and more like artists."

Sammy Cahn

The award-winning songwriter and lyricist Sammy Cahn was born in New York City on June 8, 1913. Mr. Cahn has collaborated on some of the most famous songs of his era, including "Love and Marriage" (an Emmy and Christopher award winner), "Let It Snow" (also a winner of the Emmy and Christopher awards), "Three Coins in the Fountain" (Academy Award winner for 1954), "All the Way" (Academy Award winner in 1957), "High Hopes" (Academy Award winner in 1959), and "Call Me Irresponsible" (Academy Award winner in 1963). Mr. Cahn also wrote the shows **Walking Happy, High Button Shoes,** *and* **Skyscraper.**

Mr. Cahn helped to found, and serves as the president of, the Songwriters' Hall of Fame since 1975, as well as sitting on the board of the American Society of Composers, Authors, and Publishers.

My ambition is to make eighty-seven because I want to see the year 2000, and I know the whole world will celebrate. I get my energy and force in my life from my work. It's a miracle. When I am at the typewriter, I am in a state of total happiness. When I am asked: "Which comes first, the words or the music?" I reply, "The phone call." And I don't mean that facetiously. The phone rings. Someone is calling to say that Armand Hammer is having his ninety-third birthday, and they're required to sing something. The moment they say that, all the gears go into motion and I know exactly what I am going to write. I go to the typewriter. I just put the paper in one time, type, and it's almost impeccably correct.

I was born on the Lower East Side and strove all my life to escape, and here I am, back on the East Side. I have dined with princes, presidents, and have achieved all my goals I imagined, except one: I wanted to do a cameo in a Woody Allen film.

One of my favorite pastimes is to watch all the nature programs. I watch them very carefully, because the rule of nature is the rule of life. I guess being civilized is trying to avoid the callousness of nature — the small fish being eaten by the large fish. I believe in retribution, I believe that if you hurt somebody, you will be punished. And no one has to punish you, you will punish yourself.

I waited a long time to get married. My work was my marriage, and my avocation was my lyric writing. However, one of the cruelest blows in my life was my divorce. I found myself back on the bachelor trail. I was so angry, but it wasn't all that bad. I was flying back to New York, had just taken the ring off my finger, and met this very attractive stewardess. I thought, "Well, Sam, you'd better see if the old cunning still works." So I said, "When we get off this plane, I'd like to show you my New York."

She said, "I would like to but I can't. I think I'm engaged."

Sammy Cahn

I said, "Well, if I know him, I will tell you if you're engaged. And if I don't know him, it doesn't matter."

Her answer was "Well, you know him."

"Who is he?" I asked.

"Henry Fonda."

"Henry Fonda! Lots of luck," I said. "I wish you all the nice things in life, but if it doesn't work, you'll call me?" She promised she would. And I go back to my seat. Twenty minutes later she came over and said, "I was sincere when I said I wanted to get off this plane with you and to prove it, I have a girlfriend; would you take her off?" I took her girlfriend out and we had a marvelous romance. And the other stewardess went on to marry Henry Fonda, to become Shirley Fonda.

I had the most wonderful relationships with lovely ladies, and then I met Tita. Arthur Jacobs was a good friend and he invited me to the opening of *Goodbye, Mr. Chips*. I asked a friend if she knew of someone who would want to go to the big premiere at the Palace Theater. She said, "I know the perfect girl, but she won't go out with you . . . she doesn't want to go out with transients or Hollywood people."

I said, "Just give me her phone number, please." I called her and it turned out that we had met three times before, but it had not registered. So I persuaded her to come to this opening. I must tell you she was then with Donald Brooks, the couturier, and they made her up so she looked like Cinderella going to the ball. She stole the opening. And after that night, I took her back to her apartment, I shook her hand, and I said, "I hope you had a nice time and I hope you'll be kinder to Hollywood people and transients from now on." And I left. That was the end of it for me.

Three months later, the phone rings, it's Tita Curtis inviting me to a Christmas party. I said, "Should I come alone or should I bring a girl?" She promised that there would be a lot of attractive girls there. So I brought a friend of mine, a man, and that's the day my album of my songs came out, 1969. I wrapped this album and put it under her Christmas tree. I went to the party, spent about twenty minutes, and left. The next morning the phone rings. It was Tita, and she said, "You wrote every song of my life." She discussed my songs with me in a manner that let me know she really knew my songs. I went out with her that night, and from then on we were inseparable. Tita and I got married in 1970 and have been happy ever since. My whole life is an anecdote.

I sleep very well. As I told my children, I hope I have been a good father, 'cause I don't remember any time in my life when I have woken up saying, "What can I do to hurt my children?" Not to say that I haven't. All day it seems that I am doing good deeds. Not a day goes by that I don't do something for someone. That's my code. Also, I really believe you must do a good thing for its own sake.

I have achieved so many goals, sometimes I think it is greedy to want more. I have a few Academy Awards. The first one was for "Three Coins in the Fountain," then I received an Emmy for "Love and Marriage." The second Oscar came for "All the Way," the third for "High Hopes," and the fourth for "Call Me Irresponsible." My real goal has always been to perform. When I was ten, I discovered vaudeville — a magic world. A performer, James Barton, once said: "Take stage eagerly and leave reluctantly." That is what I do. You know how performers take stage reluctantly and leave eagerly? And I say, "Why do you want to be in that business?" At the age of sixty, I danced out on a Broadway stage in a one-man show to the most incredible reviews. I did the show from 1974 till about 1980, then I started doing it only for special occasions. I

Going Strong

was asked to do two weeks in San Francisco. I said, "You find me three young singers." Instead of two weeks, they kept me there for three months. I was on a high, wasn't feeling any pain, and the reviews were sensational. And at the end the audience stood up and cheered. Then I started to run a fever. Now, if I don't show up, there's no show. They whisk me to a hospital, they give me some kind of massive antibiotic, which dehydrates me. I think I had a heart attack of some nature. The hospital said, "Look, your lungs are filled with water because your heart isn't pumping." In the meantime Tita's calling the doctor in Beverly Hills, who says, "Get him home." So we close the show and get on a plane. My doctor says, "I want you to return to San Francisco immediately to see this particular doctor." I walk into his office, and he says to his associate, "This man has given me two hours of the greatest pleasure I had in my life." I said, "You saw my show?" And he gave me the angioplasty — the balloon in the vein. He did it on Friday and I was home on Sunday. And then he said to Tita, "I want him to go back to do the show." So I did. This happened in the beginning of '89. By the end of '89 the show had become a miracle.

I get up every morning and take my medicines — I became diabetic when I was ill. I have a very light breakfast — a little orange juice with my pills, a piece of toast, some cottage cheese, and coffee. Then I go to the typewriter. Afterward, I go to the Friars Club for lunch, then on to the Warner-Chappell Music Companies, where I happily spend a couple of hours autographing my books. My songbook is a big success. Later in the afternoon, I write whatever material I have to write. As the president of the Songwriters' Hall of Fame, I'm trying to create a museum in New York City since fifty percent of the songs are written here in the city. I'm also the vice-president of ASCAP, the American Society of Composers, Authors, and Publishers.

If you want to be a songwriter, you have to have the talent and then you must build your ability by education. Oddly enough, I never finished high school. Later I realized what a terrible error I had made, because I deal in words, so I started to read voraciously. There's not a word that I don't know. I've published a rhyming dictionary of verses, but I never look in it. Today, I don't know what I would do if I were writing songs, because now the people who write the songs must also sing, publish, and record the songs as well. It's a whole different world.

I've been very ill. Before my surgery in '89, I had major surgery in '86 and almost died. I had a gangrenous gall bladder. I didn't even know I had a gall bladder. I'm a survivor and I guess I go on. My mother has an expression: "If you lie still, they will throw the earth over you. Move!" And I have another, in a song of mine: " 'Less you make a noise, 'less you make a sound, how they gonna know that you've been around?"

Peter Carter-Ruck

Peter Carter-Ruck was born on February 26, 1914. After reading for his degree in law at Oxford University, he served in the Royal Artillery from 1939 to 1944. While becoming a renowned litigator, he also served as the governor of Saint Edward's School at Oxford from 1950 to 1978, as well as the founder governor of Shiplake College at Henley. Presently, he is a senior partner at Peter Carter-Ruck Associates in London. He is on many boards and committees.

Mr. Carter-Ruck is the author of several books, among them **Libel and Slander** *(1953, third printing in 1985) and, along with Edmund Skone James,* **Copyright: Modern Law and Practice** *(1965).*

I have always been very sensitive to the feelings of other people, have considerable determination, and enjoy all sides of life. I am deeply interested in, and have always been devoted to my professional work. I also love the cinema and have made a number of amateur sixteen-millimeter films, the titling for which and the editing I have carried out myself, many of which have been shown to yacht clubs and two of which, submitted in competition, were specially commended. Over the years I have participated in over fifty offshore yacht races.

My wife is not a very good sailor but has shown great courage in crewing with me, including at least two passages across the Bay of Biscay, sailing from England to Spain.

In recent years, after giving up ocean racing, I bought several hundred acres of hill land in the Western Highlands of Scotland, having reconstructed two croft cottages there to make a further home in Scotland. I have planted over a thousand different types of trees, both there and in my home in England about thirty miles north of London, including oak, beech, Sitka spruce, lodgepole pine, sycamore, and mountain ash.

I have just completed the writing of my memoirs, covering over forty years of practice in the legal profession in England. It seems to me that to have written my memoirs in my seventies is more appropriate than writing one's memoirs in one's twenties, as has been done in the case of some of the pop stars.

My only son was killed when he was thirty-one. He was then engaged in electronic and transistor research. For a few days after that happened, we just drove around the countryside not knowing where to go or what to do. I said to my wife, "You must look forward and we must always be eternally grateful for having had a marvelous son for thirty-one years." Many people lose children when they are in their teens or even earlier. Even in tragic and difficult times, it is imperative to have a positive and forward-looking attitude.

When you have lost someone close to you, we found that it is a tremendous comfort to receive so many letters of sympathy, and this is something that those who wish to comfort their friends in such circumstances should always bear in mind. Letters of sympathy are very far from being a waste of time. It is also

Peter Carter-Ruck

important in tragic circumstances to keep one-self really fully occupied, and this is where I have felt it is always more difficult for a wife, who may unfortunately have more time to grieve because she is not working full-time whereas, more often than not, a man is engaged in his business or practice and has little time to ponder over working hours.

Being married over fifty years — we have recently celebrated our golden wedding anniversary — and having had two lovely children has been a most enjoyable part of our life.

I have had many victories over the years in conducting litigation in the High Court of Justice in England and derived great satisfaction in achieving a really good victory for clients who have suffered and thereby gain recompense. I also derive satisfaction from settling difficult disputes, both family and commercial disputes, for clients and feel strongly the relief and elation which I have brought to them.

I hold very strong feelings about injustice and consider it totally wrong that justice should ever depend upon one's means. Justice, like the right to health care, should be an equal right for every citizen and I have, over the years, been a strong supporter with many others for legal aid to be available for all proceedings for those unable to pay to be represented. I have served on a number of committees advocating this, but still legal aid is not available in a number of cases and in particular for defamation, where it is, in my view, equally important for the poor man to be able to sue to protect his good reputation where he has been defamed as it is for those with virtually unlimited means.

We do not have contingency litigation in England, though a number of solicitors, as a matter of social conscience, may be prepared to take cases on with the risk of knowing that they may not be paid.

There are two principal differences between the American law and the British law of defamation.

Under American law, one can take on contingency litigation, where the attorney taking on the case can have a contract, if successful, to take a part of the proceeds, whatever is recovered, taking nothing if the case is lost. That is not permitted under English law or procedure.

The second difference is that in the United States there is a "public figure" defense. If you are a well-known public figure, the publisher of defamatory matter can plead that what they have published is in the public interest and, although untrue, if they took every reasonable care and published in good faith, believing that what they published was true, this provides a complete defense. In short, unless in such circumstances the complainant proves malice, the publisher would succeed by pleading the "public figure" defense.

No such defense applies in English law and, unless the publication comes under the umbrella of certain specified cases where qualified privilege or absolute privilege can be pleaded, the only defense to an untrue defamatory publication, whether the complainant is a public figure or not, is truth.

My father was Victorian, strict — always immaculately dressed and a marvelous character. My parents imbued in me the precept of truth and self-discipline and to be unselfish.

Among my clients were Winston Churchill and his family, and they were always punctilious about the truth. They were also very generous.

My father always advocated moderation in all things. He also often used to say, "Don't put off 'til tomorrow what you can do today." My own life, this said, has been much more adventurous than my father's — sailing and climbing.

To keep fit and for recreation, I take a

fifteen-minute walk every morning, I play tennis and table tennis, and have sailed many thousands of miles, though I no longer own an ocean-racing yacht but crew from time to time with friends. I gave up smoking some thirty-five years ago, and for drink, I confine myself to champagne, an occasional lager, and whisky. Amusingly, the only doctor my father ever had any faith in was a doctor who prescribed that whisky was good for you.

I think it is important to keep thin and to eat sensibly and modestly. I have some fruit every day, I sleep very well, and always have a glass of hot cocoa at night. I am very active and keep fit, and I feel one must not think about one's age.

A few years ago, I said to my daughter, "I don't know whether I have as much drive as I used to have," and her reply was "Daddy, if you had more drive, we'd all be dead." Be sensible about your health. If you are going to overwork, overplay, overgamble, you are going to burn yourself out, but you can have a lot of fun and excitement without overdoing it.

I usually get up between six and six-thirty A.M. and start work between seven-thirty and eight-thirty. Two days a week I work at home and three days a week in London. One thing I won't do is to work after I cross my threshold in the evening, except to take international calls. It is very important when you reach your home to try, if possible, to put your work away and have the evening to yourself and your family. You will sleep better. On the other hand, if I have an application to make for a client the next day, I am quite willing to work all night if service to my clients so demands.

My advice to anyone going into the law as a profession is to realize that if you want to limit your working hours between nine-thirty and five-thirty P.M. each day, you will not make a success of your career. If you are prepared to work hard, give longer hours when required, give the best possible service to your client, then you can be really successful.

Barbara Cartland

Barbara Cartland, born in 1901, is the best-selling author in the world, according to the **Guinness Book of World Records.** *She published her first novel,* **Jigsaw** *(which went through five editions), at the age of twenty-one, and presently writes an average of twenty-three books a year. Barbara Cartland has several hundred books to her credit. Some of her current titles include* **Love Is a Maze** *(1989),* **A Knight in Paris** *(1989), and* **A Nightingale Sang** *(1988). In 1988, she was awarded the Gold Medal of the City of Paris for Achievement.*

I believe in reincarnation and the wheel of rebirth, so, in this life, I think you're really developing the talents which have come from another life. I'm quite certain I was Scheherazade because I love telling stories.

As I get old I realize everything which I thought at the time was disastrous turned out to be exactly right for me. I say to God that I want a plot and He gives me one within twenty-four hours. I try to write a book every fortnight. I'm in the *Guinness Book of World Records* because, for fourteen years, I've written, on the average, twenty-three books a year.

I do think that it is important to share your life with a man, the more the better. I had forty-nine proposals before I accepted the fiftieth. When I started working on the newspapers, the staff was all men. Lord Beaverbrook taught me to write. He introduced me to all the great men of our period: Sir Winston Churchill, Sir James Dunn, Lloyd George, Noel Coward, and all the people that were famous at the time, and then I was very happily married to my husband. Now it is very difficult to have six women as secretaries; I see things from a man's point of view.

My day begins at seven when the head gardener takes my dog. Then I go back to sleep. After breakfast, at quarter to nine, I sit up in bed and read eight newspapers. Newspapers and politics are what I enjoy most. At quarter past nine, my first secretary comes and opens the letters. I have forty thousand letters a year, and about thirty thousand are on health, because I am the founder of the National Association for Health. I started in 1964 as a representative for all the health shops. I receive letters asking advice. In the old days people went to see their doctor or their priest. Today, I am glad to say, they are a bit dubious of doctors, and nobody goes to their priest. As you know, religion is pale now. I'm sorry for that, because I think people need guidance all the time.

After reviewing the mail, I get up to take my dogs for a walk and clear my mind. At one o'clock, I have a quick lunch of one course and some cheese, and then go in to the library. I dictate six or seven thousand words every day, if I'm home. The secretary types back half, and the next morning, she types the rest. When I first started to write, I was advised, "If you're going to write, Barbara, write as though you're going to the office; otherwise if you wait for the muse, it never comes," so I do. I may feel ill, but I still go to the office and write — the office being a very comfortable sofa in my library.

I try all things that come into health shops, first on myself and then on my long-suffering

Barbara Cartland

family. If the products are good, I'll recommend them, and they will sell double. For beauty treatments, I consult Joseph Corvo, who also does the Royal Family. He believes if you pat your face hard enough, you'll become slim. One of my secretaries lost ten pounds in fourteen days by following his plan. He's the most extraordinary man, and I have introduced him to the world, because he was very quietly doing his grand people in the corner, and I said, "If it's known you can slim people, you'll have ten million women screaming outside the place. You've got to go public." He has this marvelous cream he has invented, for all the nutrients your body stops producing once you turn forty. And now the BBC has taken him up. He's brought out a book which is selling millions, and the BBC has created a frightfully grand video from the book. I said to him, because he is a healer, "Who do you pray to when you are healing, which saint?" and he replied, "The management, God."

Old people must be busy. The fatal thing is to stop and do nothing. People keep saying to me, "Why don't you retire?" It annoys me so much. If you retire, your brain withers. If you don't use your brain, it's like not using your hand. Only America and England are so silly as to put people over fifty in homes where they sit and look at the television until they die. They are given medicine to make them sleep. It's appalling. I think older people would make wonderful social workers. Twenty-one-year-olds don't know how to judge people, but an older person has the knowledge and can provide much understanding.

My grandfather lost all his money and shot himself. In those days, people did. But it was very tiresome. So we were very poor. Mummy, who had always been brought up in a very grand house, said to us, "Look, any fool who's got money can write a check. What you've got to do is to learn to give of yourself." My brother

then said, "I shall be the Prime Minister," and he would have been if he hadn't been killed at Dunkirk. I was brought up to give people something of myself. When Lord Beaverbrook taught me to write as a journalist, he said, "Look, Barbara, there's no use if you've got something to say to scream it on the street corner. You've got to have a platform." So I made myself a platform — morality.

In my books, my heroine is not allowed to go to bed until she is married. There are no revolting scenes with people rolling around naked on beds. I'm the best-selling author in the world. The country in which I sell the most books is France; I always thought France would want slightly soft porn, but surprisingly, they want me. I received the Gold Medal of Paris a year ago for having sold twenty-five million books in France.

My mother had the most influence on me because my father was in politics. After my grandfather crashed, my father was looking for something to do. It's awfully difficult to explain, but in those days you were brought up as a gentleman to enjoy yourself. You went riding, hunting, shooting, and fishing. Then the First World War started, and so he was called up immediately, went through four years of trenches, and then was killed in 1918. My mother died when she was ninety-eight. She was always very much in our lives.

I have been teaching a Barbara Cartland course on writing. The most important thing is to write about what you know. Don't write about gold-digging in Australia if you've never been there. People laugh and say I write about lords and ladies of large houses. That's what I know. Having had many people in love with me, I write about love and about ladies and gentlemen, which is much more glamorous than writing about the East Enders.

When people write for advice, I read their books and I always cut them down. Prose has

Going Strong

got to read as though you're reading a conversation. If you really want to write, go to your local paper and write a few stories for them. You will learn how to write quickly, to the point, and not use superfluous words. I write about moving topics.

I would like to warn young girls that it's a man's normal job to say to a girl, "You're very pretty; will you come to bed with me?" Your job is to say no. And I'll tell you exactly why. He'll say, "It's wonderful to go to bed with you but . . ." In his heart he despises you because he thinks you are easy. And when you have a row, if you do marry him or live with him, he'll throw it at you. You've got to say no.

I've been all around the world, and I've never met a man of any class, creed, color, or nationality who wants to go into a room with a woman who's his wife and the mother of his children and wonder how many other men have gone to bed with her. Get that in your head; you only give your virginity once. Don't throw it away and don't think that it's a good thing to get rid of.

I didn't set out in life to be anything in particular. Because we were so terribly poor, I thought that I'd do drawing, because I drew rather well. My first Christmas, when I was eighteen and had just come out in London, I sold menu holders on which I had drawn ladies dancing. I made twelve pounds, a lot of money then. In 1921, I wrote my first book. It went into five editions and was published in five languages. I was so lucky, it just happened.

I was brought up at different schools. I had no idea how babies were born until I had had six proposals. I was so shocked I broke off my engagement. In those days, a proposal wasn't "Darling, marry me," but "I'll shoot myself if

you won't." I was all mixed up with men and love. I was brought up as an Anglican Catholic and I was always going to church. Once in church I went to communion and I saw a Botticelli angel whilst I was saying my prayers. I knew I was being listened to. I've had lots of experiences similar to this since then. I know I shall go into the fourth dimension and not really die.

I discovered that gypsy children, since the time of Henry VIII, had never been to school because they were moved by the police every twenty-four hours. "Look," I said, "you may not like gypsies, but you have a democracy and everyone has the right to go to school." I fought a three-year battle and was very unpopular. I used to go onto the platform and was received in total silence, but I got the law changed. Every local authority has to supply camps for their own gypsies. I'm the only person in the world who's got a gypsy camp of their own. No one was a bit grateful except the gypsies. I rang the school board and said, "How are the gypsies behaving?" "They come to school clean, behave very well, and look on education as a privilege" was the reply. People who don't come from a privileged background have to fight to live and they pull a power into themselves. Everybody can do it if they want to, but also it is important to do it with control.

It's very important to always have a second honeymoon in your life. Every year go away with your husband just to make love. If you're going in a tent, it doesn't matter . . . leave the children. Even if you only have a weekend, it makes him feel masculine and romantic, and you are back to where you started. That's the way to keep your marriage alive, and that is my advice.

Leo Castelli

Leo Castelli was born in Trieste, Italy, on September 4, 1907. Mr. Castelli's first career was in banking. He moved to New York City in 1941 and joined the U.S. Army Intelligence Corps in 1944.

In 1957, the Leo Castelli Gallery in New York City opened, featuring such artists as Willem de Kooning, Robert Delaunay, Fernand Léger, and Jackson Pollock. The works of Jasper Johns, Robert Rauschenberg, Cy Twombly, and Frank Stella also had their debut at the gallery. Often referred to as the "father of Pop Art," Mr. Castelli featured such artists as Roy Lichtenstein, Andy Warhol, and James Rosenquist.

Mr. Castelli has won the New York City Mayor's Award of Honor for Arts and Culture (1976), the 1980 Manhattan Cultural Awards Prize, and in 1987, he was made a Chevalier of the Légion d'Honneur by the French government.

Art is a wonderful and supreme achievement of the human race, and it keeps me going strong. The only way you can succeed in whatever you're doing is with love and enthusiasm.

I've always felt more in tune with the younger generation than with my compadres. When I find myself with people my age that I knew in the past I find that many of them have aged terribly in spirit and I stand out as a sort of oddity in their company. Their lives in most cases just petered out and, for the most part,

Leo Castelli

they seem to be patiently waiting for them to disappear. For me life is a continuous adventure. It's a state of mind. Circumstances, of course, play an important part. I chose a lifestyle which keeps my curiosity and wonderment sharp at all times. Other art dealers no doubt share my state of mind. This profession is an aggressive one. Looking around, there are other gallery owners like myself who have enjoyed a long and fruitful life and have gone on working to the last minute. Sidney Janis died at the age of ninety-two and was very involved in his gallery until the age of ninety. Pierre Matisse, who died at eighty-five, was active to the last day. There are many examples of people in the art world who go on working because what they are doing lends itself to continuous enthusiasm. When people ask me, "Will you ever retire?" I always reply, "Of course not. Why should I stop having fun and suddenly get bored?"

My life is also very rich in all the other respects, socially and personally with regards to women, and it is still as good as it was fifty years ago. Due to various circumstances, I did not begin to find my vocation until I was around thirty years old. There were many interruptions in my life; I was uprooted and had to leave Europe and come to the United States. New York is the only place in the world where I could accomplish what I've done. I could not have been in Los Angeles or Chicago or London. I could go on working very intensely, as I do, for quite a few years. I had given myself the age of eighty to stop. When I turned eighty, I of course decided to continue.

The gallery has been through many stages since I first started it. I am still finding new artists, developing new ideas, new ways of doing things, constantly learning. I never sit back reflecting on my accomplishments and think that I've done enough. I always want to do more.

I started going to the Museum of Modern Art when I arrived in America and immediately developed a complete and unequivocal enthusiasm for art. It has to be a love affair. Otherwise you won't ever succeed.

The conditions are very different in today's art world. It used to be a much more limited world, and it had a nice, leisurely pace. Today everything's become very hectic and you have to adjust to it. It doesn't mean it's the end of art or possibilities for younger individuals. Artists will always emerge. Art is forever.

I should probably be more ruthless with my time since there are many demands on it. After each day I realize with some regret how precious it is.

I get up at eight A.M. and drive down to the gallery around ten-thirty. Each day is varied — unpredictable, with wonderful happenings as well as problems that need solving. The evening is also often dedicated to seeing people who are involved in the same pursuit I am.

In my younger years playing tennis, skiing, and *especially* mountain climbing pleased me very much. There seemed to be a higher aim there — climbing mountains, going up toward the sky. Reading was and remains very important to me. It appears that, very early on, I displayed a great ambition to learn. At the age of thirteen I started reading great literature, German, Russian, English, French in their original language. Italian, of course, is my native language, but I am just as fluent in German and French and now, English.

All my friends are involved in art, either museum activities or critics or writers, or collectors. It's important to share your life with one human being that you are very close to, and then perhaps a thousand others. I am part of a wide and warm network of friends. Even with former girlfriends, relations have remained good. And I keep track of them. We phone each other. I especially have a wonderful relationship with my divorced former wife, Diana Sutherland, who has a wonderful gallery like my own. She's seventy-six and just as young and as active at this time as ever. So you see there is yet another example that this profession seems most conducive to staying young and, more importantly, happy.

"For me life is a continuous adventure."

Philip Chandler

Philip Chandler was born in St. Louis in 1908. He has taught landscape design at the University of California, Los Angeles and Santa Barbara, in addition to Santa Monica City College, where he is currently a professor emeritus. Mr. Chandler is still actively writing, designing, teaching, and consulting.

I found my niche late in life. I have finished my first career and started something else.

During the war I was a buyer for Douglas Aircraft. As V-J day came, I thought about changing my career. I started with horticulture, and became obsessed. I went to work in a nursery. I managed to get to Kew Gardens in England for a short time, and to the New York Botanical Gardens. In 1949 I went to work for the Evans and Reeves Nursery, one of the largest and most prestigious nurseries in southern California. What I learned there was invaluable. I was sales manager, and I worked in the landscape department. In 1951 I taught in educational programs, first one night a week, and by 1960 I was teaching five nights a week. I got into more and more teaching and private consultation and eventually design.

A working day for me usually starts around nine A.M. and ends around five-thirty P.M. I go away on average four times a year for three to six days at a time, and nearly always my trips are linked with nature and visiting gardens. In the evening I meet friends or read and relax at home. I've been very fortunate to have good friends. I think it's desirable to be with someone, but I don't think it's inevitable. I lost my partner last year, who was one of my warmest friends. He was incredibly young and just getting into the prime of life.

I eat simply, mostly fruits and vegetables and relatively little meat. I go out for dinner two nights a week. I quit smoking after fifty-one years in 1980. I take iron because I get exhausted rather easily. I find working in the garden or advising on somebody else's garden very therapeutic. Retirement at age sixty-five enables people to discover a new career that they might otherwise not have had the chance to focus upon.

My philosophy is to figure out something in which you can excel, and be sure to excel.

Julia Child

The world-renowned food author and television hostess Julia Child was born on August 15, 1912, in Pasadena, California. She earned her undergraduate degree from Smith College. During World War II, from 1941 to 1945, she served with the Office of Strategic Services, the forerunner of the CIA.

Mrs. Child has enjoyed great success with her books, among them **The French Chef Cookbook** *(1968),* **From Julia Child's Kitchen** *(1975),* **Julia Child and Company** *(1978), and* **The Way to Cook** *(1989). Her PBS television series have run for many years. For over two decades, the success of Julia Child's books and television shows has opened America's mind to French cuisine.*

I am very lucky to have a good pioneer background and genes; I think that makes a great deal of difference. I'm not very philosophic, nor am I a complicated person. I don't brood and moan about myself, I've got too much to do for that. My work seems to pile up and I am never quite through with it. At least I am self-motivated.

My husband, Paul, and I have had a very happy married life. Unfortunately, at eighty-nine, he is now in a nursing home. He had a heart bypass in '76 and a little stroke during the operation, and since then he's been gradually going downhill. But, I have been prepared for it, and have now accepted this as part of life. Despite the fact that I see him every day, I nonetheless always feel guilty. When I'm out of town, there are friends who visit him regularly. As he has to have constant attention and his mind is kind of like scrambled eggs, it was better for him to be taken care of in a nursing home. In another age, with an extended family, taking care of older people was probably easier. I know so many people who have tried caring for their relatives at home, and it has almost killed them. You think you have properly organized the nursing care, but then something happens and the nurses can't come, and it gets very difficult. Also you have a responsibility to yourself. I am lucky in that Paul isn't really conscious of where he is and what's going on. I think it would be very difficult with somebody whose mind was still OK. Older people should plan for this happening to them. One is very lucky to go out like a shot, but unfortunately, I don't think many of us are going to be able to engineer that. I certainly have my end all planned so I'm not going to be a bother to anyone. When I'm eighty-six, I am going to move out to Santa Barbara, where we have a very nice condo and when I need help I can hire nurses. And then when I go bonkers it is arranged that I shall go to a specific nursing home. I like to be in control and prepare things myself.

I usually get up around five-thirty A.M., do all my exercises, and am ready to work around eight A.M. I'm involved and very much inter-

Julia Child

ested in the American Institute of Wine and Food. I was one of the co-founders, but I have been so busy on my books and television, I haven't been able to devote much time to it. I decided that this year I should pay my dues, so every time they open a new chapter, I go. Needless to say, I have been traveling around quite a bit. The American Institute of Food and Wine was established in 1981. The founders felt strongly that food, wine, and gastronomy should be considered one of the fine arts, like theater, dance, and music. For a long time, cooking has been considered blue-collar. Leaders in the wine and food business should have a very good education — languages, history, science and geography — if they are going to be leaders. We are looking toward a degree in the fine arts. Nobody else is going to make it come to pass, so we have to. Our institute is meeting with the California Culinary Academy as well as with people at Harvard/Radcliffe. So many nutritionists treat food as medicine without any sense of gastronomy. On the other hand, there are chefs who are not paying attention to nutrition. In a recent medical journal, I read a study of French eating habits. The French seem to have much less coronary heart disease than anyone else, yet indulge in eating cream, butter, and cheese. Is it the wine that helps? And does the cheese bind with something so it doesn't coat your blood vessels? These issues are fascinating to me.

I deplore this business of families' not eating together, because family meals are one of the most civilized things one can do. I think there is a breakdown in the family, not to mention the fact that a life-style in which Junior just puts something in the microwave and eats whatever and whenever he likes is very uncivilized. There should be at least one meal together during the day. What kind of people are you going to bring up if you never sit around and eat and talk and have a good time? How are you going to get along in business, or government, or diplomacy if you don't know how to receive people and entertain them? Every time the President of the United States has a foreign dignitary visit, he always entertains him or her at dinner. Whether at power business breakfasts, banquets, or special events, food is very important.

I became interested in food during World War II when Paul and I were in China. I met Paul in OSS overseas in India, China, and Ceylon. In those days, in China, the food was good. Sometimes there was a plague and we'd have to eat the army food, which was incredibly bad. I was kind of a messy thinker until Paul came along with the operational proof, scientific method. He cleaned up my thinking a great deal and helped me very much. He was a mentor to me. It was only after our marriage that I started to enjoy cooking very much. Where I grew up, it wasn't considered proper to talk about food. When Paul and I arrived in France, I couldn't get over their cuisine. From the first bite, I was enthralled. We didn't have children, so I was able to spend a great deal of time learning the fine art of cooking at the Cordon Bleu School. In 1948 I met Simone Beck, with whom I cowrote *Mastering the Art of French Cooking* (volumes I and II) and *The French Chef Cookbook*. I had been looking for a career — I'd done some writing, some publicity, but nothing had really grabbed me until I got into the food business. My French professors inspired me with their deep love and respect for food and the art of cooking. I was so fortunate in those days to receive a good classical training in what the French considered an art. Once you've learned it, you're able to cook anything, because you have the basic techniques. The French are the only people with gastronomic culinary rules.

Going Strong

My mother was lots of fun. She was far from an intellectual, but she was a loving mother and she thought we were perfectly marvelous. If I got a C minus she'd say, "Well, good. You passed!" Or if you had a D, "Well, but maybe you'll do better on the next one."

My advice to young artists: try to find what really interests you soon so that your whole life can be directed to that. I was rather late in discovering my vocation, only really after World War II.

For the everyday cook I would say: learn what you are doing. If you are going to keep house at all, you have to learn to cook, whether you are a male or a female, and I recommend taking it seriously and learning it properly. You really can't be inventive unless you have a base and know what you are doing.

"Whether at power business breakfasts, banquets, or special events, food is very important."

Henry Chung

Henry Chung was born in 1902 in China and came to the United States with his family in 1920. Mr. Chung currently lives in Los Angeles, California, where he helps to run the family business, which deals in Chinese herbs and medical remedies.

I am a very happy person with many friends, and I just love my life. What has kept me going is working all day from nine-thirty A.M. until five-thirty P.M., then I hit the bar. I do this every evening, I see all my friends, have a good time, and drink vodka-and-tonics. Another thing that has helped me are the Chinese herbs and vitamins that I take. My family has taught me how to prepare them. Ginseng and other mixtures are really good for you, and they work. I eat a lot of rattlesnake. I buy live snakes from Arizona and Texas — and then cut their heads off. I clean the rattlers and cook them with chicken and herbs; others I preserve with alcohol. Rattlesnake meat is good for rheumatism and for your whole body. You can keep the snakes for seventy years in the alcohol and herb mixture. Drinking the liquid will help you feel well. After my supper, I drink a cup of rattlesnake brandy.

My grandfather started our Chinese herb business over one hundred years ago. He passed it on to my father, and he in turn passed it on to me. Now I have handed it over to my daughter and son-in-law. I still come in every day and make up all the Chinese herbal remedies and prescriptions. It is very satisfying to be able to help people who are sick and see their health improve after having taken our remedies. A number of Caucasian people come to us to have their prescriptions filled for Chinese medicine. For a long time many people were using Chinese herbs, then there was a falling off, but now there is a return as modern pills seem not to have helped as much as was hoped.

I love America. My family came here in 1920 when I was a young man. In the Depression everyone had a bad time. I drove a truck and delivered goods. Bad times can make you a stronger person. I always knew that in this country, everything good was possible. Los Angeles is the best place to be. Since my family arrived here, we have moved the location of our shop three times.

The young Chinese in China were so brave in the uprising. I just wish the government and the people could have worked for a peaceful solution.

I think it is very important to share with your family and friends and, in my case, the customers who come to shop.

I love fishing. Maybe I do not have the pep to go out all night, but I still go on the weekends. I have fished all around the coast. What really appeals to me about fishing is the concentration that is required. When you are young, you enjoy the excitement, but at my age, I still get a thrill from it.

I could have invested in real estate and made a lot of money, but I didn't, and it does not matter because I am happy.

Clark M. Clifford

Clark M. Clifford, a lawyer and presidential aide, was born on December 25, 1906, in Fort Scott, Kansas. He began practicing law in St. Louis in 1928. During World War II, Mr. Clifford served in the Navy, becoming an aide to President Truman in 1946 through to 1950. Afterward, Mr. Clifford remained in Washington as a practicing lawyer and returned to government service as adviser to President Kennedy. In 1968 he was appointed Secretary of Defense under President Johnson. Currently, Mr. Clifford serves as director of Knight-Ridder Newspapers and Chairman of the Board of First American Bankshares, and is a senior partner at Clifford and Warnke in Washington, D.C.

I was born on December 25, 1906. My father was with the Missouri Pacific Railroad. I was born in Kansas but grew up in St. Louis, went to the public schools there, and then went to Washington University [in St. Louis] for college and law school. I have practiced law for sixty-three years. I was mainly interested in the trial phase of the law. When I reached the bar, I went to the criminal judges in St. Louis and told them I would be available to represent indigent defendants who couldn't afford a lawyer. In just a few weeks I got my first client. I defended a whole series of people, getting good trial experience. I lost the first case badly, and I continued to lose them. I must have tried fifteen of those cases, and then finally one day, I won one. Now I was not rendering a disservice to these young men, because they wouldn't have been able to get a lawyer anyway. They named a wing in jail after me the "Clifford Wing," because I was filling it up with my clients. But this enabled me then to start trying cases for the firm much sooner, because of the experience. I spent ninety percent of my time in court. I read the lives of all the famous criminal lawyers. My ambition was to be the leading trial lawyer in the Middle West. But my plans changed when World War II came. By that time, I was married with three daughters. I became increasingly uncomfortable. We got into the war in 1941. I was about thirty-five and not subject to the draft. I watched it for a while, and by 1943 it looked like it was going on forever. The Japanese were doing better in the Pacific. We also had our troops in Europe, fighting Hitler and the Third Reich. At the beginning of '44, I went into the Navy. I was out on the Pacific a good deal, and really had an exceedingly interesting naval career. Then, as the war was drawing to a close, in April of 1945, Franklin Roosevelt died.

The Vice President, former Senator Harry Truman of Missouri, became President. His naval aide was an old friend and client of mine. He sent for me, and I became the assistant naval aide in Washington. I was in the White House serving in that capacity when the war finally ended. At the beginning of 1946, President Truman called me in and said, "Clark, I want you to get out of the Navy and I want you to become counselor at the White House." That was the job I wanted. I spent four years there, during a period that was extraordinarily exciting. Those years, at the close of World War II, were to be described by some as the period that was one of the proudest periods for our

Clark M. Clifford

country in history. By the time I moved into the counsel job, the President and I had become close, so I was able to take part in those great movements. In March of 1947, the President went to Congress and delivered the Truman Doctrine message because the Soviets had increased their pressure on Greece and Turkey. Next we formed the North Atlantic Treaty Organization, a collegial group made up of the nations of Western Europe. We sent a message to the Soviets — "Attack any one of our allies and you're attacking us and it's war." NATO has kept the peace close to forty-five years. The main reason our position was so formidable was because we had the bomb. We began to reconstruct and revive and build up the Western nations. Arnold Toynbee, the great English historian, said "The twentieth century will not mainly be remembered as the century in which atomic energy was started, but the century in which the United States came to the assistance of Western Europe and saved the free world."

By 1950, I arranged a plan with the President so I could leave to practice law again. I decided since my family was now here in Washington, I should form a firm here instead of going back to St. Louis. It proved to be a wise move. I didn't let the firm get too big. That's the way I prefer to practice law. When the call came, I could go back into government.

When President Kennedy came in, I became very active again because for years he'd been a client of mine. I worked very closely with him in the campaign, preparing a fifty-page booklet on the takeover of the executive branch of the government. I spent quite a lot of time as an adviser to him, then he named me chairman of the President's Foreign Intelligence Advisory Board. He created the board after the disaster of the Bay of Pigs. I remember President Kennedy two days after that debacle, thoroughly downcast. He said, "I will not be able to survive another total tragedy of this kind. And I can see now how it came about. I

made the wrong decision because my advice was wrong. My advice was wrong because it was based upon erroneous facts, and erroneous facts were the result of faulty intelligence. I don't ever want to take that chance again. I'm appointing a ten-man board; I want them to review our whole foreign intelligence operation." I became chairman of that board and I think that we served very successfully. During the Cuban missile crisis, we had much better intelligence — not perfect, but better. And it continued to improve. After President Kennedy was killed, Lyndon Johnson took over. We were to work together for twenty years.

Vietnam became more and more of a burden. Toward the end of '67, Johnson asked me to come into the administration and serve as Secretary of Defense. I had been attending all the meetings on Vietnam and giving more than half of my time as an informal adviser. At the beginning of '68, I went to the Pentagon and worked there until the end of Johnson's administration. These were extraordinary, difficult, trying years. Nineteen sixty-eight was the year in which the war in Vietnam reached its peak. We already had five hundred twenty-five thousand American troops over there. My view was that it was a mistake for us to be in Vietnam, and I spent a lot of time attempting to persuade Johnson that we should not try to gain a military victory in Vietnam. Instead, I suggested we try to work ourselves out of it on the basis of negotiated terms. President Johnson took some very important steps toward a disengagement. However, when Nixon was elected in '68, he had a different feel about it. Under Nixon and then under Ford we stayed in for another four or five years.

Finally the Congress, in about 1973, reached the conclusion that we had a real loser on our hands, and they said, "No more money for Vietnam!" And that declaration was what finally committed us to get out.

Going Strong

After President Johnson left office in January of 1969, I returned to my firm. I've had the best of both worlds.

Young people today must consider very carefully whether they should get into law. It's a long seven years of preparing. Is it going to be what they need at the time? I started in law school on the advice of my father. He thought I should go ahead and take law anyway because it would be a splendid aid if I went into business. The men I know who have gotten degrees in law school seem better trained than those who took an ordinary general course. If you're going into law, be prepared to discipline yourself. It's a question of whether you're going to make the effort, which often means giving up everything. To become a doctor, you go through the same thing.

I have a strong personal faith. I happen to be an Episcopalian, but that is just incidental. I know that Christ lived. I know that never in human experience will there be another life like that. His philosophy was totally revolutionary at a time when cruelty in the world was accepted as the norm. He had concern for the individual and felt you should lead a life in which you do all that you can to be helpful to your fellow man. I have the deepest admiration for the philosophy that Jesus brought into the world. I'm perfectly willing to accept the theology that Christ was the Son of God. I'm concerned about what He brought to humankind. I try to instill the same attitude in my children, I think they have it. If people don't believe, it makes no difference to me. I don't care if they're Catholic or Jewish; it didn't make any difference to Jesus.

Trying cases all the time is a very stressful life. So I began to pick out those habits of life I had that I thought might, in some way, be contributing to the strain. I found the factor that bothered me. As a result, I never drank coffee again. I used to smoke eight or ten cigarettes a day, and finally began to read the messages and gradually cut down. I have one cigarette a day, after dinner. One reason I still smoke one daily is because all my friends thought I was crazy and said I could never do it. And so I wanted to prove to myself that I can, and I get a lot of enjoyment out of that one. Years ago, I found even taking an occasional drink wouldn't agree with me. I have not had a drink of any kind for thirty years. My father used to tell the story of this remarkable eighty-three-year-old man whom he asked, "To what do you attribute your remarkable preservation?" The man said, "I never touch tobacco, I never took a drink of whiskey, I never went out with a woman — until I was fourteen years old!" My life is so full and so busy that I find fewer areas of stress enable me to get through it. I went out to get my annual physical last June and my doctor, an old friend, said, "Well, how is your life?" I said, "I spend half my time as a senior member of the law firm. I spend half of my time as chairman of the board of First American Banks. I spend another half of my time writing my book." My doctor said, "You've got three halves that don't fit in the whole," and I said, "That's my problem," so I stay very busy.

This is the one chance you have, your only life. Do much with it. I would hope that as a result of this one life, others will benefit. Some people lead their lives as if they have a number of them. Old people have a tendency to be shut-ins and they shouldn't be. They can make a contribution, even if they have disabilities. If you wake up in the morning and you don't hurt anyplace, you're dead.

The deepest satisfaction in my life has been my work. I've given the greater part of myself to work. My wife understands this. She began to discover this after we were married. At first, there may have been some resentment and then after a bit she understood it. I find that if a man's happy in his work, he's very likely happy in his home.

"Rabbit" Close

Freewheeling trader and dealer John Robert ("Rabbit") Close was born in Masham, in North Yorkshire, on July 19, 1907. He will buy or sell literally anything and everything so long as it eventually earns him a profit.

I would say what's kept me going is a drop of beer. There was a Dr. Lockroft who said, "A chap that takes a pint o' beer will take no fault." My father was a very strict man. He'd say to Mother, "Hit that lad when he comes in." He'd shout, "I'll bloody kill thee," but he never would (but Mother would). I was terrified of her. Once I sat down to tea and said, "Oh, Mother, not rice pudding again." She upped and threw a bloody spoon and caught me just under the eye. It coulda blinded me easy. In them days, lads and lasses were brought up on margarine and bread. None of this fancy stuff they get nowadays. Mind you, we ate a lot of rabbit pie and sheephead. There's no man eaten more sheephead than me.

I never regretted getting married; she were a good lass. I was wed at Leyburn Registry Office and I nearly missed it, an' she was getting larger [she was pregnant]. I was in the pub with a few lads and Harry Milner said, "You wanna be off, Rabbit, else you'll miss the bus." Well, I did miss it, so I said to myself, "It don't matter." I didn't give a bugger; I was well set up. I had a horse and cart and me scrap. Anyway, I did set off walking and the Rington's tea van picked me up. I said to the missus, "You're bloody lucky I'm here." My wife would do anything for me. She wouldn't tell a lie. She was good. They were happy days. You hadn't a lot of money, but you were happy. I've seen her come home from thresh-ing and then work through the night making bread.

In life you need a partner. I've never been on my own; I'd be absolutely useless. I can't even boil a bloody kettle. I've always had somebody to look after me. Like these old men and women getting married late in life — I think it is very good, as they're company for each other. An empty house is no house at all.

I've still got an ambition to buy a headstone for my wife's grave (she's been dead for forty years). I don't even know where the grave is now. We didn't have money when she died, so I couldn't afford it. But I'm gonna do it, I'll tell you.

I don't actually go to church anymore. But I bet there isn't a man living who's watched *Songs of Praise* on TV more than me. Every Sunday without fail. I was in Masham Church choir as a boy. I've always liked "Abide with Me." They played it at my wife's funeral. Nothing made me happier than to see all the better class of people who came to see her off. Nobody believes in God more than me. I've walked up that road without a penny in my pocket, many a time, and I've said, "Oh God, help us" under my breath so no one would hear me. He's always looked after me.

There aren't many men of my age who can say, "I've never had a doctor in my life." And I thank the Lord for it.

I always kept working and always will. I've done scrap, vegetables, a bit of knacker trade,

"Rabbit" Close

dealing with horses, everything. I'll stop dealing when they carry me to Watlass churchyard. I'd get up in the middle of the night to make a deal, no bother. It keeps your hand in, keeps you interested.

I've always paid my bills. My father always said, "Pay yer rent and rates before anything else." I was in Ripon one Thursday. I'd taken some rabbit skins to sell. And I gets on with this bloke and 'e says, " 'Av you ever supped any of this Australian wine?" Well, I gets on drinkin' glasses of this stuff. Now I never remember to this day what happened, but I must have come out and fallen over in the street and fell asleep. Anyway, this big bobby picked me up. Strong bugger and carted me to police station. I said to him, "Don't put me in jail, will you?" Well, they dragged me to the courthouse and puts me in a prisoner's box, with bars on an' all. They fined me four shillings.

I was better off without education. Look what it does for 'em now. None of 'em have jobs. A schoolmaster once told me, "You've as much education as any of 'em, Rabbit. And you're sharper than most." I never brag, I just like to show a bit of profit at the end of the day. All's on credit now. In my day, if you wanted to buy sommat, you worked and saved. Them plastic cards are the worst thing that ever came out. I just deal in cash. I like cash.

If I had to inspire the youth of today, I would say, "I'd sooner see a lot of young'uns come out of a church or chapel than out of a pub." I never go to church, but I'm an old man now. I supped forty-five pints in Watlass one day, at tuppence a pint. There's no credit to that. Mind you, beer's cheaper today than it was in my day, comparing wages.

I remember the first fellow that took me to see the sea. It was just ten or fifteen years ago. I went like a bloody kid. I'd never seen the sea, ever. I said, "Oh, what a lot of bloody water!"

I'll tell you who kept me out of the war — John Broadwith. He said he wanted me as an agricultural laborer. I didn't want to go. Well, I didn't mind going; it was just the scum that you had to mix with. They dropped bombs over Masham and six or seven people were killed. A friend of mine stopped me walkin' through, on my way back from a sale. Then they dropped one on our village, Thirn. I thought I'd never see Thirn again. We hid in the coal shed, I was that bloody frightened. It killed a cow in Croft's field. By Christ, we don't want to see the likes o' that again.

We got up to some tricks in the pubs, though. A bloke put a whole box of fireworks onto the fire. Daft trick. It was Tubby Rodney. It was market day, so it was packed. Well, there was such a crack and a bang and smoke everywhere, we thought we'd been hit. Everybody ran out the pub, calling the fire brigade.

When me and the missus went down to Masham, we'd take a pram with us. I'd 'ave a few drinks. Then on the way back, past Masham Bridge, I'd get in the pram and our missus would wheel me home. I was forty-odd years old, mind you, so I took a bit of pushing. One time the gamekeeper stopped us 'coz he thought missus was poaching. He looked under the cover and found me and said, "Well, you lazy bugger."

I used to trade rabbit skins; that's where I got me name. I used to sell French letters [condoms], many hundred, many thousand. I'd go to the local dances with a basket of bananas as a blind. I've sold 'em to some good men in these dales. I got them from Leeds a gross at a time. I'd never say a bad word against 'em, they've kept my belly full many a time. They cost me tuppence and I sold 'em for sixpence. I never bothered with 'em, though.

There's really only one thing I've ever regretted, and that's not buying a house. You've a hell of a job buying land nowadays. I've no

Going Strong

regrets but that I've had a bloody good life. I've 'ad ups and downs, though. I was once in a pub in Yarn and I said, "I've had more ups and downs than any man in this place." And a bloke jumps up and says, "I'll bet you five pound you haven't had more than me." So I took him on and he stands up and he's got one leg shorter than the other. And he'd had more ups and downs than me. Never stopped going up and down. I lost the bet.

"I would say what's kept me going is a drop of beer."

Eleanore Phillips Colt

Eleanore Phillips Colt, an editor, was born on June 26, 1910, in Los Angeles, California. She began her career as the London social correspondent for the **Los Angeles Times.** *Hired by the famed Hollywood columnist Hedda Hopper to do publicity, she eventually became the head of Paramount Studio's Fashion Publicity Department. She subsequently became the West Coast editor for* **Glamour,** *followed by* **Vogue and House and Garden.** *Currently she is a consultant to all Condé Nast Publications, and in addition she serves as an associate for Sotheby's.*

*I*n the course of my life and my dealings with people, I have found it necessary as well as rewarding to try to make them feel good. In fact, it is as easy to make someone feel reassured and good as it is to destroy that person. As I was growing up, my mother, for fear I might become conceited, never once made any allusion to the fact that I was attractive. Much later, she realized her mistake and apologized. As a result of that, perhaps, I have made a point of building up those I am in contact with rather than destroying their confidence gratuitously.

My mother was very important in my life. Once a week she would take me to a Russian lady gymnast, where I did very sophisticated exercises. We also visited another woman, who taught us special breathing exercises. Back then, I was convinced that my mother was insane, because none of the other girls had to do any exercise. But I now realize how very modern, and in fact before her time, my mother

Eleanore Phillips Colt

was. Today, people are just discovering the importance and benefits of exercises and body building.

I had a very active childhood. There were all these gymnastic objects for me to play on at home: rings, acting bars, trapezes. That's probably what's kept me as strong as I am today. From the age of five on, I danced every night of my life while my mother, a marvelous pianist, played jazz and classical piano. I can still remember the tunes from the twenties. When I came home (in the summer) from boarding school in Washington, D.C., my father, who, like my mother, never thought that I should remain idle, wouldn't let us laze at the beach. Instead, I studied ballet. But today, unfortunately, I spend my life working all day and going out at night and I don't have time for daily exercise routines. Now, I only do a few exercises at home, or some neck stretches in the elevator.

I wonder what New Yorkers think of California when they come here and go to a fashion show, or to the Bistro Gardens, and see the Beverly Hills ladies with the bleached, bubble hair and the third or fourth facelift. I have been too busy to even consider having a facelift. I also believe that you have to get old at some point. Keeping alert and keeping aware of what is going on in the world is better than having a lot of surgery.

The birth of my children was a profound and miraculous experience. My strongest and happiest memories are of them — playing with them, touching them, and taking care of them. I think that in any relationship, and especially in families, love must be stressed. Life is not easy, and the more you encourage people, the stronger they become. I have no desire to quarrel or fight in relationships. Rather, I think it is best to be factual, calm, and honest.

I wasn't brought up to do anything, so,

when the Depression came, it was terribly traumatic to be suddenly out in the world and not have a penny to my name. I couldn't get a job since I wasn't trained for any specific field. An aunt of mine, one day, invited me to visit her in London. Before leaving I went to the *Los Angeles Times* and talked to Tom Trainer, a friend of the family, who was the *L.A. Times* Women's Page editor. I proposed writing articles about London. Trainer agreed that it was a good idea and told me they'd pay me by the inch. And off I went to London, with my little typewriter. (What no one knew at the time was that I had never written anything in my life!) One of my first calls was to the President of the BBC, requesting an interview. Though terrified — I couldn't type a single word — I managed to get through the interview.

During my London stay I was very busy deerstalking and going to the models' clubs every night. I also visited Biarritz and attended lots of parties there. Writing a social column for the *L.A. Times* from London was a wonderful adventure for me.

Upon my return to the States, I met Hedda Hopper, who had apparently read and liked my articles. She hired me and I became her "legwoman." I would go to Paramount Studios in the morning, RKO in the afternoon, and have lunch with one of the publicity people. They'd take me on the set and I'd try to write a story about one of their upcoming films. This was a whole new world for me. My family had never associated with theater people, believing they were all drug addicts. The editor in chief of *Town and Country,* who thought it was exciting that I worked for Hedda Hopper, wondered if she'd let me write some free-lance articles for them. Hedda agreed, and that was my next venture. Later, a woman who owned the biggest public relations firm contacted me, and I started working for one of her hotels in

Going Strong

Palm Springs as well. I didn't ever have to go out and ask for a job.

My philosophy was to let things happen naturally and to think positively. I feel that all good things happen in their own good time. They always did for me.

"All good things happen in their own good time."

Alistair Cooke

A famed British journalist, broadcaster, and host of **Masterpiece Theatre,** *Alistair Cooke was born on November 20, 1908. After studying at Cambridge, Yale, and Harvard universities, Mr. Cooke became a film critic for the BBC in 1934. Two years later, he became the London correspondent for NBC. The following year, he became the BBC's American commentator, a position he still holds. In addition to his radio career, Mr. Cooke was the American correspondent for* **The Times** *of London from 1938 to 1940, later holding the same position for* **The Guardian** *from 1948 to 1972.*

Mr. Cooke is best known in America for his television work. From 1952 to 1961, he hosted the Ford Foundation's **Omnibus** *program and went on to host* **Masterpiece Theatre** *in 1971. His documentary* **America: A Personal History of the United States** *won four Emmy awards and a Peabody Award.*

Mr. Cooke has written several books, including **Around the World in Fifty Years** *(1966),* **Talk About America** *(1968),* **Alistair Cooke's America** *(1973), and* **Masterpieces** *(1982). He has also won the Peabody Award for international reporting twice (1952, 1983) and the Benjamin Franklin Award (Royal Society of Arts) in 1973.*

PY: *Looking back over eighty years, what thoughts do you have about youth and age?*

AC: One of the few consolations of getting along in life is that at sixty you know no more than you knew at thirty, except you have a much better suspicion of the different ways people are likely to behave. The only other thing is that you get less and less sure of any-thing. Aristotle says old men, if they are extreme in anything, are extreme in moderation because "they have made mistakes themselves, they have seen many other people make mistakes and, most of all, *they have seen the pain caused by positive men.*" That's a great insight.

So I find I get less and less tolerant of ideologues, the down-the-line conservative,

Alistair Cooke

the down-the-line liberal, the down-the-line Republican/Democrat/Socialist, whatever. I more and more take to the few people who have their own position, but who can convey the impression that they may be wrong.

I'm an agnostic. I'm not an atheist. When it comes to an afterlife or the existence of a Supreme Being, I go with my old guru, H. L. Mencken. He believed he was an atheist, but when somebody said to him, "What would happen if you find yourself in heaven?" he said: "If I do fetch up with the Twelve Apostles, I shall say, 'Gentlemen, I was wrong.'"

PY: *What does God mean to you?*

AC: I do believe Christ lived as a man, a most extraordinary man. But then, there've been four or five most extraordinary men and women. The Hindus would say there've been several hundred, worthy of being called gods.

PY: *What is your regular daily routine?*

AC: My wife says I'm the most regular irregular person around. I go to bed late, I read myself to sleep. I now tend to wake up three hours later as lively as a cricket. So I read some more. I used to toss; I don't do that anymore. So I get up about nine or ten o'clock and read the paper and the magazines and then I read whatever book I'm reading (or, rather, the five books I'm reading!) and go on reading until my secretary arrives at two o'clock. From two to five it's the damn mail. I'm always five thousand letters behind. I have drawers — rooms — full of mail. You do what you can. People, especially English people, think that the "Letter" ["from America"], the BBC talk, goes only to Britain. It goes to fifty-two countries, and I get mail from most of them. Some of it is exciting, most of it is sweet and dull, a great deal of it is wild and eccentric. There are always letters from people who say, "Forgive

my writing; I'm eighty-eight" or "I'm blind." You have to answer. More than half entails rejecting invitations to talk to a foreign affairs association or the Camellia Club of Mobile, Alabama — societies of every sort — and they have to be turned down. That goes on until about four-thirty. Then I try to go for a little walk (which I hate in cities) or play some blues or a little Gershwin. Then I read till about six. Take a bath and dress up — usually down — and at about two minutes to seven I ring a mental bell for my spouse. She has her own life. She's been a professional painter — portrait painter mainly — for nearly sixty years. Everything in this room is hers, and I love it. The portrait of a granddaughter is my favorite. The best child picture Mary Cassatt never painted. Exhausted child, exhausted doll: dead to the world but both vibrant with life. We see little of each other during the day, but since I've always worked at home, that's always been the system. At seven the network news, when we approach what E. B. White called "the most beautiful sound in America: the tinkle of ice at twilight." Afterwards, we watch the *MacNeil-Lehrer News Hour*. Eight-thirty or eight-forty-five we eat. I have never worked in the evening. When I was with the *Guardian* for thirty years, I was working on the English clock, so my deadline was noon or one or two o'clock, and I got out of the habit of lunch and have never got back into it — I've escaped a multitude of bores! I eat breakfast, then nothing till a cup of tea at four-thirty. After dinner, we watch TV and then to bed, where I read myself to sleep. So, you see, I have about four sessions of reading.

PY: *What is your social life like?*

AC: I share Dr. Johnson's distaste for parties: that is to say, for more than six people in a room.

Going Strong

PY: *Tell me how you think one ought to go into broadcasting.*

AC: If you want to go into broadcasting, just try it. If you're any good, you'll bust through. I don't really believe in schools of journalism, or — God help us — "communications"! Do it! I don't think you can teach people how to write. What several people have done — the Fowler brothers, E. B. White and William Strunk, Jr. *(Elements of Style)* — and what William Safire is doing in his weekly language column is to teach people how *not* to write. These books and pieces constitute lessons in usage which alert you to the flourishing jungles of jargon so you can learn to cut through them and find your own path to clear, intelligible English.

PY: *Apart from broadcasting, you must be often asked for advice on life in general.*

AC: I don't believe in advice. All you can do is to suggest alternative courses of action, and then leave it up to them. Their character will decide anyway. So I don't think advice is any help, *except* to people whose character craves advice. There are people who cannot decide anything for themselves, and will do what an admired friend tells them. That can be dangerous — your advice may not be right for their character.

PY: *Were your parents much of an influence in your life?*

AC: Yes, but in ways probably too deep for me to know about. My mother was very intelligent, very puritanical, and very realistic. My father was very generous, very gentle — a kind, totally tolerant man. She was not. To my mother, anybody outside the church was hell-bent for the lower regions. As I grew older, I more and more leaned towards my father's view of life.

PY: *How about influences on your writing?*

AC: The first was Sir Arthur Thomas Quiller-Couch, the great "Q" — totally forgotten now. But to a little boy he was a giant, and he was the reason I chose to go to Jesus College, Cambridge, for he was then, in the late 1920s, the one and only professor of English literature. So the great day came when I lived just twenty yards away from him, and he was very good to me. He was a Cornishman, very earthy and human, very unlike the surrounding pack of pedantic dons.

There came a time when, about once a month, he'd say, "I'd like to see what you're doing." I wrote an essay once on the poet Cowper and went up to his rooms to read it to him. He was quite a dandy, dressed by day like a turn-of-the-century country squire. Now, though, he was dressing for some college feast: white tie and tails. He kept mooching in from his living room to his bedroom and he'd come back with his shirt on and his socks and shoes, no trousers, and I started reading. Eventually I came to what I knew was my great purple patch — page three — which I read as carefully as I could, because it was without question the most moving piece of prose ever written by anybody of that age. When I got to the end of it he grabbed his braces between his thumbs and said, "Cooke, you must learn to *murder your darlings!*"

It was absolutely shattering at the time. But it was the first injunction I ever had to stay with your intelligence — such as it is — and resist the temptation to be clever. There are thousands of clever writers — they jam our magazines and book reviews — highbrows: that is to say, people educated above their intelligence. So, after many years, I came to believe that whatever people think of you and your ideas, the aim is to leave absolutely no doubt what you are saying. That is the only

Alistair Cooke

great aim — clarity — especially with difficult ideas. Later still, I would say the main influences on my writing have been first, if I may dare — Aristotle. Then, E. B. White, the *New Yorker* essayist; and Mark Twain, very much; a journalist long forgotten — Westbrook Pegler, a columnist, an irascible, outrageous man but wonderful at kicking the language around. And surely, also, H. L. Mencken, the best American journalist of this century.

PY: *And your style in broadcasting?*

AC: As for my broadcast talks, I'd say I didn't really find my style until about twenty years ago. In the beginning I used to make notes throughout the week about current topics. They'd come out as miniature lectures, or surveys of the week. That's not what talking is about. So I stopped taking notes. I remembered that Freud said the unconscious has a logic all its own and I learned simply to tap mine. So the talks are really a form of free association, on a topic that's at the back of my mind, and which, during the talk, is brought to the front of it. So I never worry about what I'm going to say. It may be terribly audacious to say I know it's going to come out all right. But whatever comes to mind, don't censor it. If it is relevant to you, maybe you can make it relevant to other people. After all, broadcasting is telling a story, whether you're talking about gardening, politics, sport, history, economics, whatever. It's telling a story.

PY: *A very rewarding formula?*

AC: No, it's not really a formula: a formula is a conscious plot. However, I love it as a form of writing. I prefer it to everything else I do: books, television, articles. You can't help but be true to yourself if you're letting everything out! Obviously there are social taboos — things may occur to you that you can't say out loud (as you would on an analyst's couch), but you can learn to shave unspeakable things and make them socially acceptable.

You have to remember you are talking to one or two people in a room, preferably one. So many broadcasters, even professionals of long standing, sound as if they were addressing a PTA meeting. They pitch their voice just that much higher. And the moment you do that — change the pitch of your voice — you're actually changing your emotional attitude to an audience: you're teaching or lecturing, or talking from on high. That's not how you behave with a friend!

PY: *Do you have any rules about health — a regime?*

AC: The only thing I go on is a remark of a friend of mine at Yale who became a distinguished neurologist. He thought more people had died from what they called fresh air than anything else, so I avoid fresh air, except when it's unavoidable, on the golf course. But not my sainted wife! I go in Jane's bedroom in the morning and she has the window open. It's about thirty-four degrees in there! In my bedroom, I never have the window open in winter.

PY: *A final word, please, on happiness.*

AC: I think happiness — content is a better word — is a by-product of good work and friendship. As you get older, the best thing is friendship. Life would be very miserable without close friends. And the luckiest thing is a good marriage. It is important for me to share my life. There are people who manage not to do it. I marvel at them.

Going Strong

"At seven we approach what E. B. White called 'the most wonderful sound in America: the tinkle of ice at twilight.'"

Charles Crichton

Charles Crichton was born in England in 1910. He began his film career as an editor. Among his many successes, Mr. Crichton has directed the films **Hue and Cry, The Titfield Thunderbolt, The Lavender Hill Mob,** *and, most recently, the Academy Award–winning* **A Fish Called Wanda.**

When I am working on a film, I get up early and do an hour's preparation before going to the studio, then I spend the whole day shooting. Afterwards, I see rushes and discuss them. By the time I'm finished, it's been a long day. When all is done, I go home and have a drink. Or I have a drink before I go home. After the actual filming there's the post-production, the mixing and the music and all those things. That's not as hard as the actual production phase. You work with the editor for a day and then he goes off and tries to put into effect what you discussed.

For the beginner filmmaker or director, the cutting room is a very good place to start learning. You see how film is constructed and learn a lot about the timing of a story. You're working with material all the time, other people's material, and somehow you absorb a great deal. When I was young it was much easier to break into the field, because the business was expanding and people weren't so anxious. Films, in fact, were almost disreputable. When my auntie heard that I was going into film she said, "What a pity; he was a nice boy." Now it's hard to enter the film business. I believe in

Charles Crichton

film schools, but they're not perfect. I've had occasion to teach in them myself, and I'm very proud to see the kids who have become directors. It's exciting to see them succeed. Those kids who really have some talent in them can benefit from school. But you can't just learn to edit or direct or act from a course; there's got to be talent inside you in the first place. The competition in the industry is very severe.

I decided I wanted to go into films when I was at Oxford. I think it is essential to take a break between school and university. After school, I came to Canada and was a prospector up north. They offered me a permanent job, so I wrote to my father and told him I was going to stay in Canada. He quite rightly said that I could go to Canada anytime but I couldn't go to Oxford anytime, so would I please come back to England. I returned. During my last term at Oxford, the Kordas were making a film. I went to see them and got a job with Zoltan Korda in the cutting room. Two days after graduating from Oxford, I was in the cutting room. I was very lucky and moved up very fast; I was an editor within two years. When the war began, I went into the reserve because I was doing propaganda work. In 1943 I was making small propaganda films, so therefore I was an editor for only eleven years. And then I became a director, which was quite nice.

I think you're hiding yourself when you make comedy. When things are terrible it's much easier to have a joke about it than to be serious. I've always loved comedy and read a great deal of it when I was a kid. I just loved the director René Clair and his comedy.

My father was a businessman, and he had a very inquiring mind. I was filing some old letters the other day and read that when he married my mother they lived in a closed Presbyterian society — he went to the minister to find out whether Hester, my mother, would talk to him. The minister wrote a letter explaining he'd spoken to Hester and thought my father had a very good chance. Now I can't imagine my father doing this! The father I knew was the one who went off to the war, got wounded, had a mistress in France while he was married, and no one knew about it. My father in 1918 was quite different from the man who had approached the minister before the war. My father's advice to me was to marry either a French girl or a Scot. He liked French girls and Scots; my mother was Scot, and his mistress was French. He was pushing me constantly in many directions. I had to read the *New Statesman* every week, and I didn't have the faintest idea what it was about. Everyone in the family had to play different musical instruments; we had an orchestra.

People think and tell me that it must have been fun making *A Fish Called Wanda*. When you are completely involved in the making of a film it can sometimes be very draining rather than fun. I think the word *satisfied* is a better word than *fun*. One feels tired and satisfied when one's done something that works.

Human relationships are the most important in the world. While we were making *A Fish Called Wanda* I became good friends with Jamie Lee Curtis and Kevin Kline and all the people working on the picture.

My wife gives me pills which she thinks will keep me alive a little bit longer. But my advice to everybody is to smoke as much as they want, drink as much as they want, and to have a good relationship with a woman — or several women. . . .

I never sit around and brood about myself. I'd rather not, for I feel if I started to psychoanalyze and indulge in self-exploration, I might very well start to go downhill.

Going Strong

"If I started to psychoanalyze and indulge in self-exploration, I might very well start to go downhill."

Quentin Crisp

The British author Quentin Crisp was born on December 25, 1908, in Surrey, England. Mr. Crisp is the author of ten books, including **The Naked Civil Servant, How to Become a Virgin, How to Have a Lifestyle,** *and* **Manners from Heaven.** *He has also contributed articles to such magazines as* **House and Garden** *and* **Lear's.** *In addition to his writing, Mr. Crisp has acted in a number of television roles and had a feature role in the movie* **The Bride.** *Mr. Crisp moved permanently to the United States in 1981.*

I haven't much energy these days. I only write books people ask me to write.

People who are always busy don't have to think about their lives, or fate. Lately, I have had a lot of spare time, and plenty of time to think about myself.

You should find out who you are, and what your purpose is, and when you find out, you then should go about fulfilling your goal.

It is a great mistake to get tied down to a job that simply requires getting up, putting on the right clothes, taking the right train, and giving the right answers. This kind of routined existence is what makes people so old, so angry, so tired.

I'm lucky, I never had to participate in the predictable nine-to-five world. At first, when I could not find a "real" job, I felt unlucky, but I've realized that actually I live in an ideal state. I wouldn't consider my writing real work. I do have to organize my thoughts and sit here in my room with my typewriter on my knees and type. Even when I am performing on a very small stage, it doesn't feel like working. Someone once said to me after a show, "Are you very tired?" And I responded, "I don't think

Quentin Crisp

anybody is allowed to say he is tired after doing two hours of work a day."

I've always kept busy. Since I was incapable of doing "real" work, I first assisted a printer in an art department. Then I began to write books. I was about twenty-six when I wrote my first book, about lettering. Next, I wrote a book on the art of window dressing, and others followed. Nothing (big) happened until I wrote the story of my life, *The Naked Civil Servant*, in 1966; it was published two years later. I was amazed when I learned that it was going to be made into a film. I thought it was a joke.

For thirty-five years I was also a model at the art school, while at the same time acting in the theater. I've been in Sting's movie *The Bride* and on television a number of times. Now, I write for magazines such as *House and Garden* and *Lear's*. I'll review books whenever I am asked.

I don't do anything in my spare time other than recharge my batteries by sitting in my room and doing nothing. And when I am not in my room I am with the world, observing, being observed, talking to people, and answering any questions they wish to ask.

I have frequently seen programs on TV on the problems of retirement, but there is no problem; you just retire. The thing is if you have to work, never get so identified with your job so that the idea of not being there becomes appalling. Try and be identified with your idea of yourself. This you can be whether you are working or not working. It is important to learn how to use your leisure, and to look forward to the time when you'll have a lot of spare time and think of ways to enjoy it.

My mother had the greatest influence on me. My father hardly ever spoke. So he was no influence in my life.

When you get old you don't sleep such long hours. I get up and I walk around the room and make a cup of tea. I wait until I feel I'm allowed to type. Living in a rooming house, I wouldn't want other people to hear the typewriter when they are still asleep. By ten A.M. I start to type until I get tired of that. I don't think I ever work longer at any one thing than between ten A.M. and one P.M. and two or three to five or six P.M. If possible I leave what I have written until the following day in order to get a little distance. Everything I write has to be written at least twice.

I have never believed in that health obsession. The word *cholesterol* had not been invented when I was young, and I am here, age eighty-one, and eat what I want. Like most English people, I love bland food. I have no particular regime. I eat when I am hungry and I work when I must.

As you get older, you also get slower. You can't help but regret the passing of your looks. Nobody ever mentions that when asked about old age. The first thing you lose is your looks. They no longer can be used as a weapon — to save you or to get what you want — and you have to learn to do without them. The main thing is to learn not to go on as if you were younger than you are. If you are not careful, you do it without knowing.

Coming to America is the most wonderful thing that ever happened to me. I always wanted to come, but I couldn't pay my fare, so I could only come when I was invited. And then I set out to become a part-time American, which I am now.

The people in America are so different from the people elsewhere. They have done more for me than the English ever did when I was young. The Americans have been marvelous.

I was a victim of people's prejudices in England, but perhaps I connived that without realizing it. In America, that appears to have changed. I live in the same way, in one room, in a rooming house, and go about the world by myself, and only once have I been threatened in the streets of New York in the eight and a half years I have lived here. In England I was always worried when I was outdoors. The difference is that when the English don't like something they say so and if they do like something, they don't say very much. It would embarrass them to say, "I think you're marvelous." In America it's the reverse. They pay you compliments the moment they see you.

I love Americans because they are for you, on your side. They encourage you and hardly ever vent their rage on you. In America, if you say you are preparing an act, everybody will say, "Would you like the name of my agent?" "What are you going to wear?" "What are you going to sing?" In England, if you say, "I am getting up an act," someone will say, "Oh, for God's sake, don't make a fool of yourself." In England the pursuit of success is considered vulgar; in America it is taken as absolutely natural.

I did a show in Los Angeles and loved it there because everybody is beautiful and rich. All the women are actresses and all the men are lawyers. Americans do worry a lot about becoming older. And this is partly because everything is geared to the idea of being beautiful and desirable. Your sex life is fulfilled by driving the right car, drinking the right wine, and wearing the right perfume. Then the day comes when none of these things apply. The advantage of growing old is that as it's towards the end of the run you can overact appallingly and not give a damn.

I imagine other people imagining me as always having a certain attitude towards life. The only thing I take seriously is my relationship with the world. I try not to make promises I can't keep; I try to keep my part of the bargain. Unfortunately, you can't always do it. Politeness is important to me: I don't mean bowing or scraping or eating with the right fork, and knowing how to address a cardinal, but trying to accommodate people. Saint Teresa said, "We must treat all people as if they were at least better than ourselves" — that is wonderful, and I think we should all try to live that way.

Freddie de Cordova

Freddie de Cordova, award-winning producer of **The Tonight Show,** *was born in New York City on October 27, 1910. After graduating from Northwestern University and Harvard Law School, he entered the theatrical world, working as an assistant in the Shubert office. In 1943, Mr. de Cordova began working as a film producer and director for Warner Brothers, and in 1948, he moved to Universal International. He became one of the pioneers of live television show production when he moved to CBS in 1953, guiding three of the most popular series ever:* **The Burns and Allen Show, The Jack Benny Program,** *and* **My Three Sons.** *Mr. de Cordova today produces* **The Tonight Show** *on NBC. His work for that show has earned him six Emmy awards in 1963, 1968, 1976, 1977, 1978, 1979.*

Shoot for as high a mark as you can. If that perfect situation doesn't work out, be content and do something else. I've had this remarkable job for twenty years.

After I finished Northwestern, I went to Harvard Law School. There, I had the good fortune to be in the same class with John Shubert — the only son of the Shuberts who owned all the theaters all over America. One day John asked me whether I would be going ahead and practicing law or would I like to come into the Shubert office as his assistant? I could have kissed him. Here I had an opportunity to work not only in show business, but with the heir apparent to the entire theatrical world. Since then, I have never had a day off salary, even though often enough some of the salaries were not enough to feed me.

If you can combine health, happiness, and good relationships with people, you are very lucky. To be in the right place at the right time is vitally important. I thank God for making it happen.

I have never learned to shake my Catholic background and a belief that there is a God. It would be depressing to think that it was all

Freddie de Cordova

over the moment you close your eyes. For good or for bad, the Catholic church really instills in the young a belief in God that is unlikely to dissipate, no matter how raucous your life is. On stressful days, I find myself saying some of the prayers I was taught as a child.

Some of us feel that we have been kind of blessed. While most of my life has not necessarily been ecstasy, it's been in the main very pleasant. One of the things that has pleased me the most was a close relationship with my parents until they died in their eighties. We were a very tight-knit family. I miss them. When events happen today, I still think of them as the only two people with whom I could laugh or cry together about it. I didn't get married until I was fifty-three years old and have been happily so for over twenty-six years. My relationships with my parents and with my wife are somewhat similar and have provided me with support and happiness.

My mother and father lived on the edge of the law most of their lives. My father was, you might say, a con man, and my mother his very capable assistant. The last ten or fifteen years of my parents' lives, I was affluent enough to have a family get-together and say, "All right, we've lived high on the hog during these experiences of yours, Dad, but now I'm making enough money. I retire you both to a life of honesty." Both of them started to applaud, and for the last ten or fifteen years of their lives they were totally straight and enjoyed it. My grateful father said to me, "One of the nicest things you've ever done to pay me back for the love I gave you is for me to spend the last twenty years of my life not having to look over my shoulder."

My mother and I adored my father. If there was a ball game I wanted to go to and there was a concert he wanted to go to, he'd say, "Well, there'll be another concert. Let's go to the ball game, son." He was a very dear man

with a good sense of humor. I often think back on how much fun I had with him. He also insisted on a good education and proper table manners. I remember his strong hand with love.

As a result of my father always brushing with the law, I grew up firmly believing in scrupulous honesty. I believe anybody who steps one foot out of the line of honesty, both in relationships and with the law, is a fool. My major precept is — be totally honest. My precept number two is to be as decent with people as you possibly can. If you try hard, the extra phone call you make or the extra letter you write pays off.

Happiness is doing what you like to do. I have been blessed with a series of circumstances that allow me to do most of the things I have wanted in life. Some brilliant person once said, "If you can't do what you want, want what you can do."

As far as health is concerned, I have done many of the things you are not supposed to do, drank a lot of vodka and smoked cigarettes and did very little exercise. This combination of vices seems to have kept me healthy.

I intend to go to work for as many years as I can. Not every day is fun when one works, but working is exciting. The best thing about going on a vacation is when you come back to a job. Just having a continuing vacation would be meaningless.

If you crowd the most activity into a twenty-four-hour period, and then repeat that the next day, and again and again, you'll find that a week and then a month and then a year and God knows how long has gone by while you've kept yourself busy.

I have enjoyed damn near everything in my life. I get up at seven-thirty A.M. and read as many newspapers and magazines as I can, so I am always ready when [Johnny] Carson asks me a question. At ten A.M., I meet with the bookers — the people who book the guests for the show. At eleven A.M., I have a meeting with the production staff to go over the details of that night's show. At noon, I get the bookers together with the production people and we discuss anything that needs to be known about that night's production and future guests who may have demands, transportation or hotel. At two P.M., there's a secondary booking meeting to discuss future shows, sometimes as far as six months or a year in advance. At three P.M., rehearsals begin, and I go downstairs to watch what's happening under the aegis of the director and get a sense about the details of the show. At four-fifteen P.M., there is a general meeting with everybody involved in the show. We do the show at five-thirty P.M., and it's over at six-thirty. Then we go to Carson's office and discuss what was good, what was bad, what we should have done. I then drive home. My wife will ask me, "Did you have a pleasant day?" and I will answer yes and then she'll tell me, "Good, well, hurry up because we are going out tonight." I'll let her know I'm very tired and she'll promise that "it will be an early evening." Since I start work every morning at seven-thirty, it's got to be an early evening.

Sometimes I think it's totally impossible to really get started in show business, but people do every day. No matter what facet of show business you are in, show it to somebody, whether it's on a street corner or the Elks Lodge. Get in front of whatever public you can find. It doesn't mean that you go directly from the street corner to Broadway, but if you sit at home and tell yourself you have a great deal of talent, you will get nowhere. The same goes for writing. If you write something and think it's amusing or profound, get it to the neighborhood newspaper. Don't jump right away to *Time* or *Newsweek* or *Spy.* The odds on becoming a success in show business may be minimal, but they expand if you make the effort to show people your talent.

Noah E. Derrick

Noah E. Derrick was born in 1889 in Cedar Grove Community, Lexington County, South Carolina. Mr. Derrick taught in local schools before serving in the United States Army during World War I.

Mr. Derrick has been the president of the South Carolina Association of CPAs as well as worked for the American Institute of CPAs. In 1965, Mr. Derrick published a history of the first fifty years of the South Carolina Association of CPAs.

Keeping busy and following my natural instinct have given me my energy. People who retire at sixty-five years of age and sit around the house probably die prematurely. I keep moving and still go to the office. My work has kept me going, and I've always been active in all aspects of life.

While I don't deal with clients right now, I do read all the tax journals, as tax is my primary interest.

I have always maintained what people call a positive attitude and felt that, no matter what, there would be a better day. By working hard and continuously, I achieved certain results that have helped me lead a fulfilling and consistent life.

I was brought up in a home without a great amount of wealth; as a result a simple way of life seems to have suited me best.

I've been in the accounting business for seventy-eight years, and I'm the senior partner in the Columbia CPA firm of Derrick, Stubbs and Smith. It's exciting to me and a source of great pride to be doing work today for the descendants of my clients, dating back to 1919. Their fathers and grandfathers were my clients.

When I began in this field, we had to learn accounting as best we could from available books, solving our own problems as we went along. The only equipment we had was a manual typewriter and what passed for an adding machine.

The greatest pleasure in my life was the birth of my daughter. Sadly, she died when she was one year old. I can still remember her vividly. My love for her taught me to love the rest of humanity and to be more compassionate.

Harriet Doerr

Harriet Doerr was born in Pasadena, California, in 1910. She attended both Smith College and Stanford University. Since 1978, she has taught and participated in Stanford's Graduate Fiction Program.

Harriet Doerr published her first novel, the critically-acclaimed **Stones for Ibarra** *in 1983. She has also won the* **Transatlantic Review** *Henfield Foundation Award, as well as a grant from the National Endowment for the Arts. Ms. Doerr is currently working on her second novel.*

When I was a child, no one tried to make me conform to anyone else's ideas. I could disagree or say anything short of four-letter words. I was never told: "No, you're wrong. You must try to think this!" My father died when I was eleven, so my mother had the more profound effect on my development. She was a wonderful person and used to laugh when we argued with each other. I am extremely grateful to her for letting us grow up unfettered; she looked at us as these odd creatures a generation removed from her and didn't try to mold us. Of course, there were standards. We grew up learning to be kind and thoughtful. But we could read and think anything we wanted.

Writing reveals you to yourself. You discover things quite by chance. The words are

Harriet Doerr

on the page and you ask yourself, "Is that what I think?" An enormous amount of writing and invention comes out of the subconscious. My writing evolves from what I observe, experience, remember, and imagine. My style is defined by how these elements are combined. The fine line between memory and imagination is nearly invisible, and often, "where fact ends, truth begins." The goal, though, is always to write fiction that provokes readers and provides them with insight.

One of my favorite times was when I lived in Mexico. Mexico was like a gift being handed to me. My husband's father left a mining and lumber property to his family. He eventually took on this mine in a tiny village where we were the only Americans. It was totally different for me, as I was born in Pasadena. The Mexican people are a combination of the most extreme sophistication and a sort of innocence at the same time, a wonderful stoicism without being gloomy about it. It was a marvelous experience for me. We started out with a house that was falling apart.

About ten percent of *Stones for Ibarra* is autobiographical. I loved having my book published, also the experiences which led up to it — eight years of being with people two generations younger than myself. It was marvelous and any rigid, tight parts of me, like schedules and doing beds the right way, everything got looser after that. The rest of it is made up. The book has been translated into Spanish by Octavio Paz. That pleased me a great deal.

I always loved to write. After I was married, I was in a kind of a housewives' amateur writers' group. We would read to each other the pieces we wrote. I only became serious about my writing after my husband died. My children challenged me to go back to college and graduate, and I took an undergraduate writing course at Scripps College.

In the course of a writers' conference where I happened to mention that I had gone back to college at sixty-five when I became a widow — after having been married for forty-two years — I was asked if I had been happy for all those years. I answered that no one could claim to have enjoyed an uninterrupted "happiness" for such a long period of time, or else such a person wouldn't be writing a book.

It's the ups and downs that make the happiness possible. It's not supposed to be some constant apple pie. I was happy when the book was published. I didn't think I would ever finish writing it or that it would be published. I feel a little bit that way about the book I am writing now. You can't help but think about how much time you have left.

Sharing your life with someone is very important. There's nothing wrong with me right now that having a man in love with me wouldn't cure. I suppose that most people would find such a remark for an eighty-year-old woman surprising. Women need a man to love them, at any age. I'm probably too old to have sex. My husband died when I was sixty-two, so the subject did not arise. Now I have turned antisocial; it's the only way I can get work done.

Don't let anything lie fallow. Use everything you have. Whatever your talent is — gardening, planting, painting, words, music — don't just shake your head. Try at any age! I am terrified with my second book. When I went to college first time around, very few women went to work, and I didn't formulate my future in any specific way. There weren't all these women's jobs. Women didn't train, except for the few who wanted to become chemists or scientific. It sounds ridiculous in today's thinking, but all we expected was to get married and have children. That was the only career we were looking forward to.

I am a determined person. There have been hard times when I felt like throwing in the towel, but I didn't. As a widow, you need time to grieve.

Going Strong

It's much better to look at your life and come to terms with it instead of dreaming. I consider myself lucky that I wrote my book and that it was published. But a little more than luck is involved. I have one birthday wish: to hold on to my memory, imagination, curiosity, energy, and love for words for another year. However, just to love would suffice.

"Don't let anything lie fallow. Use everything you have."

Enrico Donati

Enrico Donati was born in Milan, Italy, on February 2, 1909. He came to the United States in 1934 and became a citizen in 1945. Originally, Mr. Donati studied economics and social sciences at the University of Pavia, from which he graduated in 1929. However, art always being his passion, he pursued painting in Paris, and joined the Surrealist group, with which he remained affiliated until 1950. Parallel to his career as an artist, Mr. Donati has managed the international French perfume company Houbigant, Inc. He presently owns the company and serves as chairman of the board.

Mr. Donati's works are displayed in museums all over the world, including the Museum of Modern Art and the Whitney Museum in New York and the Galleria Nazionale d'Arte Moderne in Rome and in Milan. Mr. Donati is a decorated Cavaliere Della Corona D'Italia.

The most important aspect of my life and what I have most enjoyed is working. I also know that both my commitment and total involvement in my work are what have kept me going strong and young.

While I had an urge to create, it was imperative that I earn a living. I had to compromise. I ended up dividing my life in two parts, by going to the office in the morning and then to my studio and staying there until evening. That pattern never changed. A very good friend of mine, Marcel Duchamp, knew of my double life. "Should I pursue being involved in two works at the same time?" I asked Duchamp. And he replied, "Absolutely, because if you give up your work of the morning, you'll never come to the studio with the ambition and the desire to get rid of all the rest." He encouraged me to keep this kind of a pattern. Later on, I became involved in the art and architecture department at Yale University, and I was on the President's Council of Yale for seven years. My career, at that time, started to divide itself in three parts: one was the work; the other was the teaching; and the third was the work in the studio.

Enrico Donati

I started my career at Houbigant (the French perfume company) when I was a young man of twenty-five. A year later I was fired. In 1950, the owners called me back and asked me to look into their affairs and help them out. They made me chairman of the company, and then when they wanted to get rid of Houbigant, I bought it.

As an artist, my aim is to create something that will last long after my death.

In the art world, I became one of the boys of the Surrealist world of Paris. It gives me pleasure to see people look for my old work. I remember Duchamp also saying to me: "You have to see it while you're alive."

As for the business side of my life, I had to rebuild a company that was completely down. It was a challenge. I operated by instinct, not from the books, and it has worked. What I did to rebuild the company and bring it back to something interesting gave me the opportunity to be elected to the Hall of Fame of the perfume industry. That was a great recognition. But nevertheless, I didn't take it too seriously. I am happier to get recognition as an artist from art critics.

I have kept the same work routine I started as a young man. I get up at seven A.M., leave about eight, and work at Houbigant until about noon. The work consists of everything from marketing to advertising to designing to running the entire organization. After that, I go to my studio. It's my wonderful escape. I'll paint until dinner, go home and then go back and work until midnight or one A.M. I'll work Saturday and Sunday, Christmas Day, New Year's. Nothing stops me. I have found a wonderful person in my wife, Del, who helps me, encourages me, and is not jealous of my creative talent.

My art has evolved tremendously. From the Surrealist world I moved into something entirely different, and I created a style now recognized by my fellow artists and collectors. Since the '50s, I have been fascinated by fossils. The fossil carries the whole cycle of creation, destruction, and rebirth within it. This is essentially what I try to show in my work — the mystery, power, and indestructibility of life.

I don't want to relinquish any part of my activities. That is what keeps me alive and going and young.

My health regime consists of eating very little and being trim. I smoke a pipe but I don't inhale. I don't drink at all. In the morning I take a vitamin that is ordered by my wife, but I don't like to get involved with medication.

My father was a professor and a great lawyer. His bible was the Napoleonic Code. He used to read it like a book, a dictionary. I got from him the pattern of being really serious about what I'm trying to do.

Don't be fearful to go back to school. It's never too late to get involved.

There is no limit to what a person can become; the only thing required is willpower. Merely making money doesn't mean a thing to me.

I came to America with twenty-seven dollars in my pocket and two children to raise. I never doubted that I could overcome a lot of obstacles. I used to paint in my kitchen because I didn't have a studio. I kept on painting, and it kept me as happy as if I'd had a lot of money. Freedom is very important to me, not only the freedom of the body but of the mind.

America has tremendous potential for young people if they know how to capture it. I think they are too channeled into certain directions. If they go to college, after college young people feel that they have to take a master's. Then because they have mastered that subject, they pursue it. There are openings everywhere. The exploration of what's happening to the right and the left is as important as the street you're walking on.

Going Strong

When I was very young, as I was working with a model in my studio, I realized that people don't look enough. They look at an arm, a hand, certain curves, but they really don't see them. Look from behind the retina and not strictly with the eye but with something that you feel. If you feel the color at that time, you make it in your drawing. You can create a life around it. If you just look at it and try to draw, all that will come out is an arm with a line going one way and the other going the other way. The old masters — Leonardo, Michelangelo — when they were doing hands and arms, looked at them from behind the retina. They knew if somebody was feeling hurt, feeling love, feeling satisfaction, feeling a smile coming to them. One has to be able to read those looks.

"I don't want to relinquish any part of my activities."

William Draper

William Draper was born in Hopedale, Massachusetts, on December 24, 1912. He studied at Harvard. Throughout the 1930s he was involved in the Art Students League. During World War II, Mr. Draper served as one of five official combat artists in the United States Navy.

Mr. Draper has painted the official state portraits of John F. Kennedy, Richard Nixon, the Shah of Iran, Kings Faisal and Saud of Saudi Arabia as well as a number of business and society figures. In addition, he has three works decorating Bancroft Hall at the United States Naval Academy.

I am an optimist. Whenever I have been down, I've always thought things would get better. My philosophy of life is not terribly deep.

I hardly ever think about dying, although I have had some near misses. For example, when I was in the Navy as a combat artist, I was in a plane with my squad leader on a pre-dawn takeoff when suddenly over a loud-speaker a voice announced, "Draper, get out of the plane." I got out of the plane, and the plane was shot down.

I just live and have a good time. I paint and go along from day to day. I do a bit of exercise, ride the bicycle I have at home. Whenever I am in the Caribbean, I love to snorkel. The only vitamin I take is Vitamin E. I gave up smoking thirty years ago. I never wanted to start smoking, but everybody at school called me a sissy for not doing so. I ended up smoking two and a half packs a day. If I hadn't given up smoking, I might not be here. Don't be weak and let your peers influence you.

My wife left me after twenty-five years of marriage. She wanted to paint and be some-body herself. At first, I was very upset, but then after about a year I started going out. I loved ballroom dancing, so a friend and I would give demonstrations in Hyannis Port. Afterwards, people from Arthur Murray's Dance Company asked us to teach. Now, I'm asked out by a lot of ladies who enjoy dancing. I've also studied ballet because I wanted to paint it. I went to the School of American Ballet and I'd jump, leap, and pirouette and my glasses would fly off.

I still try to paint every day. If you want to be a painter, the most important thing is to paint every day. I want my paintings to look as if they were done easily. They are not, but when I am finished they should give that illusion. As a portrait painter, I always observe color, such as the difference in the color of a forehead or a neck. If you just use one flesh color, your painting will look like a wax model. My advice is that if you are painting somebody, be sure to get your proportions accurate. Jump all around on the canvas, just build up; you can cut in with a background or cut it out; the face will evolve.

Alfred Eisenstaedt

Alfred Eisenstaedt was born in 1898 in Dirschau, Germany (now Tczew, Poland). He began his career in 1929 at the Berlin office of Pacific and Atlantic Photos, as a special photography representative. In 1936, **Life** *magazine hired him as a staff photographer, and he has remained with the magazine since then.*

Mr. Eisenstaedt has won many prestigious awards: in 1951 he was named Photographer of the Year by both the **Encyclopaedia Britannica** *and the* **University of Missouri.** *In 1988 he won the Master Photography Award given by the International Center of Photography, and in 1989 he was presented with the National Medal of the Arts by President Bush.*

Mr. Eisenstaedt is the author of several books, including **Witness to Our Time** *(1966),* **The Eye of Eisenstaedt** *(1968),* **Eisenstaedt on Eisenstaedt** *(1985),* **Eisenstaedt: Martha's Vineyard** *(1988), and* **Eisenstaedt: Remembrances** *(1990).*

---

*B*eing a fanatic has given me my energy and creative force. An uncle had given me a camera when I was twelve and I experimented with it until 1916, when, at age eighteen, I was drafted into the German army. I was wounded in 1918, and it was not until around 1925 that I was able to resume photography again. I became a full-fledged photographer in 1929, in Germany. These were bad times in Germany since the Hitler regime was gaining power.

When I arrived in the United States, in November 1935, my work was already well known worldwide. I was able to work with Mr. Luce right away for a new magazine called *X*.

I never want to retire. In 1989, a Dr. Controwitz from Harvard Medical School called me. He had read in the *Boston Globe* about my arthritis and that I was handicapped and couldn't work anymore. He was writing a book on the subject and asked to interview me.

Alfred Eisenstaedt

When I told him the doctors had warned that nothing could be done for me, his reaction was "You're absolutely wrong; I'll find you the right doctor." And he did. I went to the doctor he recommended and discovered that all the exercises I had been doing were wrong. Now a physical therapist, suggested by Dr. Controwitz, comes twice a month to stretch my legs and give me physical exercise. Later, I suffered extreme vertigo, and similarly, a neurologist told me that my situation was impossible; nothing could be done about my loss of balance. Again, Dr. Controwitz came to my rescue, and located a physician who helped my condition. This last doctor told me, "When you get older, this tablet replaces a lost chemical in your brain." This year I will be ninety-three.

My reliable and good memory has always helped me. On rereading my diaries, I marvel at the richness of my life. I used to work day and night for *Life* magazine. I would come home at three A.M., and return to *Life* at eight in the morning, where I would often be told: "Tomorrow morning you are to leave for Washington," then, "No, sorry, it's changed. You leave this afternoon." I've learned not to postpone anything. If somebody tells me to do something, I do it right away.

Now, my working day begins at nine-fifteen A.M. and I stop at three P.M. I come to the *Life* offices every day except Saturday and Sunday. I sit on the terrace on the eighth floor for an hour and sun myself, I also try to eat my lunch there: lettuce and a pinch of herbs that my sister-in-law has prepared for me. I was always a health nut. However, after my wife passed away, I ate all the wrong food, and in 1982, I suffered a mild heart attack. Now I've returned to eating correctly, thanks to my sister-in-law, who lives in the same building as I do, and cooks for me in the evening. I can't have salt, and can eat very little red meat, so I mostly eat vegetables and chicken.

I'm currently preparing pictures for two new exhibitions. One exhibition opens in Martha's Vineyard with a big champagne reception for seven hundred people. Later at the International Center of Photography in Manhattan, there's another exhibition of seventy-five of my pictures, an autograph party for my new book, and a slide lecture. My fourteenth book is coming out soon.

I have photographed so many people in my long life and remember many encounters with them. Hemingway was a most uncooperative man. He used bad language all the time and needed to show that he was stronger than me. He displayed a false macho kind of attitude. I liked Kennedy. Bertrand Russell reminded me of a crocodile. He was like a stone. In 1933 I photographed Goebbels. He looked and spoke to me in a very angry way. I photographed Marlene Dietrich three times: once in 1928, and again in 1929 and 1953. The first time was in the commissary in Hollywood at Fox. I photographed her eating. Then I photographed her with John Gielgud and Noel Coward at the opening of the Bolshoi Ballet, Prokoviev's *Romeo and Juliet*. Sophia Loren was definitely my favorite. I did about six covers of her. She was wonderful, right from the beginning. She always treated me like a member of her family; and when you are a member of her family, everything is done for you. Recently I photographed Mr. Reginald Brack, the president of *Time* magazine, with a hand-held camera — I never use strobe lights. The pictures came out beautifully.

I receive so many letters asking for advice and autographs. But I sign only my pictures and books. And now I have a lady who answers all of my letters because I am too busy.

My advice to young photographers today is to learn how to see; never ignore what your senses tell you. Technique comes later. When I am photographing, I never push people around. If someone tells me he can't be photographed now, I try to convince him. But if he persists, I won't do it. I don't steal pictures.

That is maybe why people always call me back and remain friends with me.

How do I want to be remembered? As the man who photographed the sailor kissing his girl in Times Square.

"Being a fanatic has given me my energy and creative force."

Milton Feher

The international dancer Milton Feher was born in 1912. During his long professional career, he performed with both the Ballets Russes de Monte Carlo and the George M. Cohan Company. In 1945, he founded the Milton Feher School of Dance and Relaxation of New York City, which he still runs today.

Knowing that I have my feet on the ground, both literally and metaphorically, makes my whole life more secure. I have a creative force under my feet — the support of Mother Earth. What keeps me going strong is the knowledge that it is always possible to improve and that one's body can be put into a better position of unity with the mind.

My work revitalizes me. According to my method, if you feel effort in any exercise, it's wrong. Until 1946 I was a professional dancer on Broadway in famous long-running shows like *Song of Norway*, George M. Cohan's *I'd Rather Be Right* and *Sons of Fun*. During that time I worked very hard to become the greatest dancer in the world.

One morning I woke up with my knees pulsing and hurting and discovered I had arthritis. It was caused from the stress of incorrect dancing. Orthopedists, osteopaths, and chiropractors failed to help and advised me to give up dancing. Desperately, I tried to help myself. I didn't know I could reverse it until I started to think about the importance of posture. In order to have what I considered a perfect posture, I would tighten my muscles

Milton Feher

strongly, and that gave me control, but also caused stress. I didn't realize the negative results until in one performance I was dancing a particularly difficult solo. From the audience I heard a child exclaim, "He's working so hard!" It came as a shock to me.

That was precisely what I didn't want. The effort was showing. I learned that time that when you're balancing on one leg, you should use no muscle tension — only the resting of the mind and body.

My youngest pupil in the school where I teach dance is twenty-four. My oldest pupil, Claire Willi, is ninety-nine and a great inspiration. She has been attending my classes for twenty-eight years. She came to me when she was seventy and feeling old. She never took a walk for pleasure because her feet hurt. She wore a little pillow under her dress to hide an extreme swayback. Now her back is the straightest in the class and she goes for a walk in Central Park after her dance class. Her attitude is that she can constantly learn more to improve her body and to walk better. Recently she was delighted to learn a new exercise I devised to make her posture straighter.

Since then she has been telling her many admirers, "If you would like good posture at ninety-nine, bend your head and trunk backward every day to defeat the habit of bending forward too much."

When you relax, so many functions are helped. One of my pupils, who has been hard of hearing from birth, hears better when she relaxes. Other pupils see better when they relax. My arthritis, in other words, triggered a whole new approach toward helping myself, and through that, other dancers. I've had no pains in my knees for forty years.

In 1946 I studied the Alexander Technique but soon discarded it, finding it too strenuous. Dr. Edmund Jacobson's book *Progressive Relax-ation* was also very helpful. But the best thing was finding the right balance to relax. That balance allows the weight of the body to be governed by gravity. If you're standing on one foot, gravity will take the weight of your trunk and put it on your base, which is your foot.

Orthopedists have sent people to me with backache, arthritis, and muscle problems because our relaxed way eases these conditions. Another doctor, from Johns Hopkins Hospital, sent hundreds of his cerebral palsy patients to me. I also had many students with polio.

When I see people in pain and see a possibility of helping them, I derive the greatest feeling of fulfillment.

If I am going strong at seventy-seven, it is largely because my wife, Margo, is great fun to be with and a great partner. She has transformed a dance studio into an oasis of peace; its beauty inspires my pupils and myself. The next great joy I have is dancing. It is enormously satisfying for the body to feel lighter and flexible as one grows older.

The potential of a relaxed body is enormous. Most of the time our bodies are too tense. The head is too far forward, causing more and more strain. When your head is not balanced over your shoulders it causes stress throughout the body. One should remember that a relaxed body straightens out by itself. Don't *work* to improve your body; just relax. I've been researching relaxation since 1946, and there is not a day that I don't discover new tensions that I have not known before.

A few months ago a doctor informed me that a little bump in my mouth was possibly cancerous and might require serious surgery. It turned out to be all right, but for two weeks I was anguished, feeling certain that my work was ruined, and that I would have to stop teaching. During that stressful period, however, I worked to improve my relaxation more than ever. As I lay there with the thought of my whole life's work being halted, I let my arms rest, and my head and trunk sink down and my legs relax. My body immediately felt better, more comfortable. It really helped. I had another cancer two years ago. I was operated on and I am fine today. I was given a very strong anesthesia and it took time for my strength to return.

Throughout my various misfortunes, I've relentlessly told myself: "Make the best of it."

And because I always turn bad news into good, my wife once pleaded, "Can't we, for once, live through a simple straightforward disaster without turning it into a good thing?"

"What keeps me going is the knowledge that it is always possible to improve."

John Kenneth Galbraith

John Kenneth Galbraith was born on October 15, 1908, in Ontario, Canada. Considered one of the most important liberal economists of this century, he taught at Harvard University from 1949 to 1975 as the Paul M. Warburg Professor of Economics. In 1961, Professor Galbraith took a three-year leave from Harvard University to act as the United States Ambassador to India, appointed to that post by President Kennedy. Presently he is Professor Emeritus at Harvard and lives in Cambridge, Massachusetts.

Mr. Galbraith has written more than a dozen works on American political and economic thought, including **The Great Crash** *(1955),* **The Affluent Society** *(1958),* **The Age of Uncertainty** *(1975, with Nicole Salinger),* **The Anatomy of Power** *(1983), and* **A Tenured Professor** *(1990).*

I've allowed life to take over as it comes. I would like to think I had a long-run design, but I'd have considerable difficulty persuading anybody this was true. I've never had a seriously bad time and I've always believed, as everybody else does, that time has its own healing qualities.

The most important thing for me is to have a sense of compassion for people who are less fortunate. This is not only good for the soul, but it's good for survival. Elites in the past have shown a singular capacity to protect themselves from the alienation and anger of the less fortunate.

The most important thing I learned from my father was that you can have a reasonably varied life, and one of the variations should be a certain concern for public affairs, public well-being. If anything went wrong in the community, my father felt personally responsible.

John Kenneth Galbraith

Because I saw his public commitment as well as his ability to do a great many things at the same time, I've always tried to escape narrow specialization. My father brought me up as an old-school Baptist. My instincts, in consequence, are slightly on the secular side. To this day I can't go in St. Peter's or St. Paul's without being afraid that some preacher will capture me.

My wife and I were married in 1937 and lived happily ever after. We enjoyed our years in India. If you go to Europe, it's a variation on life in the United States. But in India, it's something totally different.

I just published a novel called *A Tenured Professor*, which seems to have met with general approval. And I am currently outlining a book on economics and politics, which I am going to write next. Nothing is quite so boring for me as a vacation.

I get a certain amount of pleasure out of finishing and seeing one of my books published. I have a wonderful capacity for deciding that good reviews are deeply percipient and bad reviews are somehow unfounded and ludicrous.

The Affluent Society was published in 1958. It was a book which, for the first time, indicated that the economics and the politics of a comparatively wealthy country might be different from those of a poor country, that we had to make an accommodation to the fact that many Americans were comfortably off, and also that a distressingly large number of Americans still hadn't made it. And I think the situation has not changed much. Help to the homeless has been cut back and as a result, there are more of them on the street and more discussion of their plight in the newspapers. No one should doubt that we're doing much less than we have in the past. We also now know that quite a lot of our recent housing expenditure got diverted into the pockets of politically influential people.

For people as they go on into the world at large, I have one piece of advice, which I always give: you have only one life to live, and it is far too important to spend working on the extremely dull business of just making money.

My life, I suppose, has been a fairly open book. I have always kept secret a certain wish, a certain wonder as to why I never ran for public office, having advised a lot of other people to do so. I suppose a kind of natural, instinctive caution that has caused me to be strongly — and perhaps properly — concerned with the likelihood that I would lose. In retrospect, I wish I had tried.

Diplomacy is a very agreeable and important profession. As to the danger, being an ambassador is safer, on the whole, than driving your own car in California. My strongest advice is not to assume that all wisdom emanates from the State Department. You cannot escape the need to think for yourself and occasionally annoy your superiors in Washington.

I was brought up to believe that one didn't go to heaven unless one took some exercise every day. I try slightly to control the amount I eat. But I find that I almost invariably postpone that resolution until the next meal.

My mother died when I was still in high school — so it was indubitably my father who influenced me. He was for much of my life my only parent. And he was quite a wonderful man. He combined the life of a farmer with that of a public servant and political leader. And he even ran a small insurance company.

I was very close to a professor here at Harvard by the name of John D. Black, who was one of the founders of the subject of agricultural economics. He brought me to Harvard, and when I went away during the war, he brought me back afterward. I'm not sure he was a mentor, but I live in continuing gratitude for what he did for me. I've had lots of students and have given them much guidance, but I'm not sure I'd call myself a mentor. I don't feel I can take that much responsibility for any student's success.

"I've always believed, as everybody else does, that time has its own healing qualities."

Sir John Gielgud

The world-renowned British actor Sir John Gielgud was born on April 14, 1904. After studies at the Royal Academy of Dramatic Art, he began his career in London, starring in several plays during the 1920s and 1930s. Sir John has also appeared in many movies, including **Richard III** *(1955),* **Becket** *(1964),* **The Shoes of the Fisherman** *(1968),* **Chariots of Fire** *(1981), and* **Arthur** *(1981), for the last of which he won an Academy Award for Best Supporting Actor.*

Sir John's many other awards include being made a Knight of the British Empire, a Companion of Honor, and a Chevalier in the Légion d'Honneur. His books include **Distinguished Company** *(1972) and* **Gielgud: An Actor and His Time** *(1980).*

Sir John Gielgud felt that the Bard said it all:

To thine own self be true,
And it must follow, as the night the day,
Thou canst not then be false to any man.

The undiscover'd country from whose bourn
No traveller returns, puzzles the will,
And makes us rather bear those ills we have
Than fly to others that we know not of . . .

There's a special providence in the fall of a sparrow. If it be now, 'tis not to come; if it be not to come, it will be now; if it be not now, yet it will come: the readiness is all. Since no man has aught of what he leaves, what is 't to leave betimes? Let be.

Sounds and sweet airs, that give delight, and hurt not.

And this our life exempt from public haunt,
Finds tongues in trees, books in the running brooks,
Sermons in stones, and good in every thing.

I am myself indifferent honest; but yet I could accuse me of such things that it were better my mother had not borne me. . . . What should such fellows as I do crawling between heaven and earth? We are arrant knaves, all; believe none of us.

Charles Gingerich

Charles Gingerich was born in Stuttgart, Arkansas, on January 13, 1914, and is currently the president and CEO of Gingerich Draperies, Inc. The client list for his custom-made curtains and draperies boasts such names as Ronald Reagan, Richard Nixon, the White House, Jack Benny, Joan Crawford, Marilyn Monroe, Michael Douglas, and the producer Aaron Spelling.

I think young and work hard and enjoy. I try to concentrate and reflect on things past and future and conduct myself as I have been trained and taught over the years. My parents were both deeply religious people in the Methodist church. I was a Sunday school teacher and I directed the church choir for a couple of years in my late teens. I am a firm believer in God. As far as I'm concerned, He is the Architect and Builder of our universe. In adverse circumstances, my religious background and training, family relationships, and love have kept me going.

I graduated from high school when I was sixteen and it was the Depression years. I had hoped to go into medicine. I went to college and stayed at my mother's sister's in Memphis for two or three semesters. Things were so horrible financially that I just couldn't swing it. So I went to work to help with the family and I never got back to school.

I fell into this drapery business by visiting Los Angeles when I was stationed up in Oakland.

I enlisted the beginning of 1942 and went through boot camp in Williamsburg, Virginia, as a First Class Petty Officer. At the Marine base, Camp Lejeune in North Carolina, someone chose me to go to an advanced Military Intelligence School with Marine officers, of all things. They had me set up a Military Intelligence School for the Seabees and as the officers came back from the war area in the Pacific, they came to my school.

I was divorced during the war and remarried in 1951. We had a daughter and I was delighted. From my first marriage I had two sons who were both Annapolis graduates, and I am very proud of them. Now I have nine grandchildren, and my oldest granddaughter is expecting, so I'll be a great grandfather.

I admired and respected both my parents. They imbued in me honesty and congeniality and sincerity and doing your best, all influential to my longevity. The Golden Rule is a personal formula that I try and follow. "Anything worth doing is worth doing well" is my motto.

Lord Lew Grade

The pioneer British film producer Lew Grade was born in 1906. After a brief career as a professional dancer, he entered the television and film business. Among the many films he's produced are **Sophie's Choice, On Golden Pond,** *and the* **Pink Panther** *series. In addition, Grade has produced for television the acclaimed miniseries* **Jesus of Nazareth** *and over a hundred episodes of* **The Muppet Show.** *Still a leading media mogul, he is currently producing Barbara Cartland romances for television films.*

In 1976, Lew Grade was made Baron Grade of Elstree by Queen Elizabeth, and in 1979 he was decorated a Knight Commander, Order of St. Silvestre, by Pope John Paul II.

I'm eighty-four and I'm just starting. People used to think that when you were sixty, you were past it. That's nonsense. As long as you can think, you've got to keep going. The busier you are, the better you feel.

I measure wealth by the number of friends you have. In which case, I'm the richest man in the world. You have to treat everybody equal, whether it's the dustman in the road or the chairman of a top corporation. Relationships are the only thing that count, and the reward of building relationships and friendships is great satisfaction to me.

I'm very fortunate. I have a wonderful wife. She believes that nothing is impossible for me to achieve. Without my wife I'd be a goner.

Lord Lew Grade

She's my whole life. She works with me, puts up with me. I'm very nervous and she always manages to calm me down.

I love the business of television and movies and theater. It's a wonderful feeling when things work. When Barbara Cartland saw the first of the films I am presently making, she cried with pleasure. In fact, her son, Ian McCorquodale, thanked me and told me: "Lew, you've given my mother at least another ten years of life." That was a great feeling of satisfaction.

In 1926, at the Royal Albert Hall, I became the world's Charleston champion. To my shock and horror I found out later that the judges were Fred Astaire and Charles B. Cochran. My prize was four weeks at Christmas at the Piccadilly Hotel. What a wonderful way to earn a living — dancing for four minutes. Afterwards, I became a professional dancer. But I could see that eventually there was no long-term career for me. Can you imagine me doing the Charleston at seventy? Yet I still do it. And then I went into television and movies. I founded independent television. On my eightieth birthday, I had a surprise: *Variety*, the American trade paper, did a special issue as a tribute to me. That thrilled me. And it was a remarkable tribute as well to all my friends like Franco Zeffirelli, who so beautifully directed *Jesus of Nazareth*. That film is my greatest achievement. Zeffirelli is such an inspirational artist.

My mother always told me never to lie, and I don't. When somebody asks me: "What does this picture cost you?" rather than making up some false figure, I reply, "I'd rather not tell you."

I'm enjoying life more than I ever have before — because I'm making two or three films a year as well as developing some others.

Three years ago I had an angioplasty — they clear one of your arteries with a balloon kind of treatment — and as a result, I feel great.

I get to the office around seven o'clock in the morning, every day. I read scripts and make a lot of phone calls to California, Japan, Hong Kong, and New York. I see people, plan. The important thing to make a film work, apart from the script being right, is to cast the right star for the right role. If casting isn't done correctly, you lose the whole texture of film.

For those young people who want to become producers, I should warn them that it's a very difficult and trying business. But if you believe in it, it's worth pursuing. My advice for breaking into the field is to start by contacting the top person in charge of development at production companies. Share any ideas you have. You can't just say, "I want to be a producer!" It takes hard work. You might be unlucky at first but if you persist, something will eventually happen. When I decided to do *On Golden Pond*, it had been turned down by all the studios, but I nonetheless obstinately felt the chemistry was there. The rest is history. *On Golden Pond* was one of my huge successes along with *Sophie's Choice*, and the *Pink Panther* films.

I've never worried about money — all I wanted was to have enough for cigars, food, and an occasional new suit. And my wife, who works very hard for numerous charities, is very understanding.

My blood pressure is perfect and my cholesterol count normal. I have very little breakfast — a biscuit and a cup of tea. Never had butter in my life, nor cheese. It's a problem at cocktail parties, because most of the cocktail hors d'oeuvres contain butter. So I stay hungry. But sometimes I weaken and indulge in too much ice cream. I don't take vitamins. I don't drink. I do smoke cigars, Monte Cristos, all the time.

I enjoy life and people. The word *retirement*

Going Strong

should be removed from the dictionary. Keep on working, remain active, in whatever field you choose. Never give up. It's important to do something you love. I love the entertainment industry, particularly television. And I'll go on forever, I hope.

"I'm eighty-four and I'm just starting."

Kitty Carlisle Hart

Actress and arts administrator Kitty Carlisle Hart was born in New Orleans on September 3, 1915. She studied at both the London School of Economics and the Royal Academy of Dramatic Arts, and has appeared in many theater and film productions, including the Marx Brothers' **A Night at the Opera** *in 1936 and* **On Your Toes,** *which ran on Broadway from 1983 to 1984. Kitty Carlisle Hart wrote her autobiography,* **Kitty,** *in 1988 and currently serves as chairwoman of the New York State Council on the Arts. In addition, she has resumed her role as a guest panelist on NBC's revival of the classic quiz show* **To Tell the Truth.**

Writing a book, which I did very late in life, helped me learn a great deal about myself. I discovered hidden feelings I was still harboring about my mother. Writing enabled me to look at her and the difficulties she had faced in her life. When her husband died, she had no trade and no money. Despite great difficulties, she was raising her child, trying to educate her in the finer things of life. Only then did I understand what she had been faced with. When the book was finished, my enormous admiration and love for her overcame any previous resentment. My mother was larger than life.

My days vary because I travel a great deal. I lead two or three different lives. The Arts Council takes up about ninety percent of my time. I go to an office and deal with personnel, getting money, going to legislature, setting up budgets. I also spend a great deal of time with my friends and family. I sing and I lecture around the country about art or my life. I find that very rewarding.

If I didn't have a public service job like the one I am involved in now, I would find an occupation that would be helpful to other people, such as working with children, or in a hospital. I couldn't live a life just for myself.

I haven't always been altruistic. When my husband, Moss, died in Palm Springs I was left alone with these two little children looking at me with big eyes saying, "Mama, make a life." I came back to New York and participated in a weekly television show, *To Tell the Truth.* I seemed to be on every board in town. I worked in the governor's office as a volunteer on "Opportunities for Women." That position led to the Arts Council. Ever since I became a widow in 1961, I've been involved with some kind of volunteer work or public service.

I have always enjoyed working. However, what made me the most happy was when Moss asked me to marry him. Life with him was wonderful. Everywhere he went, he brought the excitement of life up at least ten notches. Bennett Cerf [a distinguished publisher and editor, cofounder of Random House] once said, "When Moss walks into a party, the party's made." That's the way it was living with him.

I believe in exercise. As a singer, your instrument is inside your body. But it needs to be well maintained. I drink only a little alcohol. When I feel the beginning of depression coming on, I either get out and take a walk, or count my blessings. I can always find something to be grateful for. My recommendation

Kitty Carlisle Hart

is: snap yourself out of it as fast as you can.

When I get up in the morning and don't feel very cheerful, I fall back on a silly little trick: I always smile at myself in the mirror. I try keeping that smile on for the rest of the day. I believe that one can change one's mood and one's attitude from the outside in. If you start to smile, you get a better reaction from the people around you than if you show a gloomy, grouchy face. Whenever I keep smiling, things always get a little better. My work and my friends have been my mainstays after I lost my love.

I was put on the stage by my mother. In my day, very few girls had careers. They didn't even go to college in Europe; they went to finishing school. Then they got married. I had no role models for work. In my group, you aimed to marry a rich aristocrat; that was the extent of your ambition. Failing that, you married a poor one. I went on the stage in order to find the right husband; that's what my mother told me. Once I got to RADA, the Royal Academy of Dramatic Art, I discovered that acting was the one thing in the world I really wanted to do. My mother really loved the fact that I adored the stage and I was willing to work hard to be an actress.

Singing is a cheerful occupation. After you've finished singing an hour or more, you feel exhilarated. It is a great therapeutic outlet. I know very few singers who have ever committed suicide. Now, Judy Garland had such a bad upbringing that maybe she did, but I can't think of any other singers who ever killed themselves.

Nobody can ever visualize the end of the road. But about four years ago, I saw it extremely clearly, without fear and without sadness. It was simply there. I suddenly thought, "My Lord, the little annoyances are so short in terms of one's whole life span, why allow anything to take away the joy in being alive?" I used to push taxis over the stoplight. I would

be so irritated if I was late or if somebody was late for an appointment or a dinner guest dropped out. If the plane's late and you're due for dinner, unless it's life-and-death, what difference does it make really in the long run? Young people never think they are going to die. I don't think I'm immortal anymore, and that makes life a lot easier.

My father was a doctor. He died when I was ten years old. I can remember his face from photographs. If I needed something for a fever, he would make a crease in the bottom of the paper, shake the powder down to the end, put it on my tongue and then give me a piece of candy to go down afterward.

Getting started in the entertainment business is Catch-22. When you begin your career you must have an agent. But in order to get an agent you have to get a job so he can see you. If I were to counsel young aspiring performers, actors, singers, I would say that unless you think you're going to die if you don't go on the stage, don't do it. It's tough, it's disappointing, and the statistics are going against you, so very few people succeed.

My mother taught me never to give up a dream. One thing that has helped me to keep going is my inability to know when I'm licked. I never seem to know; I just keep on going.

Never say you don't remember names anymore. Don't let it come into your consciousness. If names do escape you, squeeze yourself, force yourself to remember. You will. Never stop working; if you do the brain will go to sleep. I remember a couple of years ago I decided to do two plays in summer stock just to see if I could memorize both of them. Memory is a muscle and if you don't exercise it, it will vanish. I think it's a good idea to memorize something every day, even if it's only a small couplet.

Moss tried dictating his work into a machine. When he got the transcripts back he said, "It's not writing. It's verbose, it's repetitive, it's talking." He couldn't write plays like that. Moss wrote longhand. He used to sit on the terrace and write. He would look up from the paper, mouth the sentences out loud that he had just written in order to hear the rhythm of the speech. He spoke every line to see if it had the right balance and the right snap for the joke. He was a terrific director; he directed me marvelously and taught me a great deal. I'd been in vaudeville most of the time before I was directed by Moss. The first play I did he said to me, "Honey, you don't have to face the audience to get the laugh." I said, "You don't? Well, in vaudeville you do." He said, "No, you get the laugh if you talk to the person you're supposed to be talking to."

Now my life is of complete involvement. I am fulfilled. Each morning I wake up and say, "Dear Lord, I don't want anything better; just send me more of the same."

"Whenever I keep smiling, things always get a little better."

Sir Anthony Havelock-Allan

Sir Anthony Havelock-Allan, one of the most important producers involved with the development and growth of British cinema and television, was born on February 28, 1904. Beginning in 1924, Sir Anthony worked as an artists' and recording manager for the Brunswick Gramophone Company in London. Later he worked for Vox AG in Berlin in the same capacity. In 1933, he became a casting director and producer's assistant for a number of studios, including Paramount, Pinebrook, and Two Cities Films. In 1941, Sir Anthony served as Noel Coward's producer. The following year, he joined with partners David Lean and Ronald Neame to found Cineguild. Sir Anthony has produced such films as **Brief Encounter, Great Expectations, Oliver Twist, The Quare Fellow, Othello,** *and Zeffirelli's* **Romeo and Juliet.**

What has kept me going strong is a passionate interest in cinema and world events. Politics have always been very important. Some of my family have been members of Parliament and I have participated in political life.

A visual imagination fuels my life force. From childhood on, I have collected paintings: landscapes and, later, old masters. My mind and my memory are intensely visual. My creative energy has derived from that stimulation.

I don't dwell on my misfortunes but rather examine them to see if something positive and life-affirming can be extracted from any given experience.

I was a lonely child and spent a great deal of my life by myself, and during that time, I tried to find out why I do what I do and why I think what I think. I've learned a great deal about myself. If I had had that knowledge of myself earlier, I would have worked much harder and spent much more time looking for stories that were worth making into films.

I've made a lot of films in my life. A great many of the early ones were pure potboilers.

I made twenty-three "quota quickies" for Paramount Pictures in a couple of years. All of them were an hour and a quarter long and all of them cost exactly one pound a foot. Terence Rattigan and Robert Morley did scripts for me. These little films shown in the cinema at ten o'clock in the morning, with no audience, were made to fulfill the Quota Act, and to match the number of American films that were on show. I've never had more fun, and I learned a great deal about the cinema.

Left-wing governments are always rather favorable to the film business. Right-wing governments look upon the entertainment business rather as people in the time of Queen Elizabeth looked on actors. They are very entertaining but not very serious or reliable and they're liable to spend too much money. The advantage of the British cinema is that we share a language with the Americans. The disadvantage is that our whole market consists of only just over a thousand cinemas whereas the American home market consists of seventeen thousand. There is no way you can recoup the cost of a film made here, in this small market.

Sir Anthony Havelock-Allan

You must have a success outside and the answer is in America.

We have no backing from the government. France, Germany, and Italy have backing. It would be the most helpful if the government would give some tax advantages to bankers, to induce them to invest in film.

I am working with two writers on a script to be filmed in Vienna. It will be an E.E.C. coproduction. I'm waiting really for the European Community to start because it will be looking for European subjects, and this film fits that category. It should soon be in perfect shape.

The voices of the film industry — France, Italy, and Germany — are for the first time speaking with one common voice, saying, "Look, for many, many years the Americans have had the run of our cinemas and the major viewing time. Now we want it."

I've always thought in terms of film. I'm just as able-bodied as I was, and all my faculties are still with me. I hear less well, but that's no great barrier to making films. Unfortunately, the film business is thought of as a young man's business and anybody of my age who has a project is likely to encounter that prejudice, particularly in America. But I know I will produce this film and it is immensely pleasurable making the preparations.

The only advice I can give any young filmmaker is, if you really seriously want to work at nothing else, get a start somewhere, TV, video, documentaries, or commercial filmmaking . . . it's not easy to get in because there are union difficulties, but if you really want to do it, you will find a way. This is the most fascinating business that anybody can ever work in because with each film, you are creating a new product and working with new people. It's not like making a product that you see in a shop window. You can experience your creation when you sit in a theater and you feel whether the people like it or not.

I'm used to going to different organizations such as Rank or British Lion and saying, "This is what I want to make. This is who I want to write the script. And this is who I would like to get to play in it. Do you want to put up the money?" And that's the only kind of producing I've ever known and understood. Now I have to adjust to the present climate.

While we were making the film *Ryan's Daughter*, five different owners of Metro were there. They never asked any questions or said: This is costing too much.

Making *Brief Encounter* was one of the most fulfilling periods of my life, because, when we made it, we looked at it and said, "Well, if we had to do it again, we wouldn't know how to do anything differently. What we set out to do, we appear to have done, and if nobody wants to see it, that's too bad."

I think the wonderful thing about God is that the human race was able to invent Him. I have no clear idea whether there is such an individual, but I am absolutely clear that there is such a force that makes people sometimes much greater than what they really are.

I had a coronary, in 1966, and I was told I should take up walking. I was in the hospital for two months. I still try and walk, come hell and high water, for an hour a day. I never had a robust constitution. I've had a great many operations and quite a few illnesses, but I'm in good shape for my age, and I attribute that fact to two things: At the age of fifty I gave up smoking, and I drink fairly moderately. I don't think I've been drunk for twenty years. I also eat very modestly. There are certain things your body begins to tell you. It's one of the things you learn when you get older. The name of the game when you are old is feeling well. If you don't feel well, it's very boring. And there is always that lurking suspicion, if you don't feel well: "This is the thing which has come to take me away."

Going Strong

If you take certain risks when you are old, you probably won't survive. A lot of old people are troubled because we live in a very violent world. Your instinct, if you see violence being done on someone else, is to do something about it. My instinct would be to try and stop it. But I am equally conscious that the hardest punch I can launch is about as hard as being hit by a butterfly, so I would probably not survive. I pray God that no one will molest some girl, that no one will attack a weaker human being, and that I will not find myself going to the rescue, because it would be a disaster.

I was brought up in the dower house of a fairly large estate that belonged to my uncle. The next-door estate belonged to my mother's family. We were pretty pampered. My old grandmothers had been members in the royal household.

I thought I was a grand young man until the age of eight. After the war I went out to debutante parties and to the last ball at Grosvenor, Norfolk, and Bridgewater houses when they were private residences. I thought I was one of the elite, which of course I wasn't at all, because I had no money and nobody really remembered who you were before the war. I got the feeling that I was very much a member of the establishment, which I also wasn't at all.

The class system is changing enormously. It is just one of the things that make political life much more difficult here than in America. As far as the upper classes are concerned, they now marry absolutely anywhere, and it's very good and will produce much better and livelier children. Class differences are reflected also in boss-employee relationships, which doesn't happen in America because there an employee not only thinks he's as good as the boss, but always thinks he can become the boss. One of the sad things in England is that accents and voices do distinguish people, but it's becoming much rarer. There are now a lot of upper-class children who deliberately speak with Cockney accents.

I have always truly loved life. I read a great deal. When I was a child, during difficult periods, my mother would say: "Well, after all, my family did come over with the Conqueror." Which was quite untrue. From her I felt that I could conquer any adversity.

When I was growing up it was unthinkable to do many of the things that the youth of today do and take for granted: being untidy, or rude to older people, or unkind or brutal. The moment young people were able to be independent of their parents, and the moment both parents started working, the whole structure of the family went, and the whole structure of authority disappeared.

I went to schools where you were beaten very soundly and thoroughly for any transgressions. That helped. Now, if you were feeling very rebellious you might well do something, but you knew there was a penalty. There is no penalty anymore. I don't think it harmed any of us. I think it is the removal of authority that has loosened everything so that anybody can do anything now. As a result, we have a great deal of violence.

My advice is, if you haven't got a passion, try to find some kind of love of life, because there is much to be loved in human nature. Think of Mother Teresa, or someone else who is doing good works helping other people. Follow their example of giving. You don't have to be a saint to help make the world a little better.

Milt ("The Judge") Hinton

"Judge" Hinton was born in Mississippi in 1910 and grew up in the Midwest. Throughout his career, Mr. Hinton has played with some of the greatest big-band, bebop, and modern jazz musicians ever, including Cab Calloway, Count Basie, Louis Armstrong, and John Coltrane. His book **Bass Line** *is a record of his life on the road with his fellow musicians.*

I attribute my force and energy to music. Like most young boys, I was always in trouble. When my mom would banish me, I would take my violin, go off by myself, and play and try to create. Being sent away was therefore solace, never a punishment. It was a way for me to find out about myself and my feelings. What I discovered was that nobody could ever take music away from me.

In those days, there were a great many injustices happening to young black kids. No matter how unfair the conditions were, I knew I had my music. As I grew up I played in different bands; I was able to get by. Football players were popular with the girls in football season; the baseball players in their season, but a musician was popular all year round. Being a musician, I felt special, somehow above the crowd, and this sense of confidence helped me in my relationships with girls.

I also discovered the universal language of music. You don't have to speak the language of another country to know it's the same note in China as it is here. In 1953 I was with Louis Armstrong in Japan and, in spite of the war, the people really welcomed us. I recently returned from playing in Finland and in France. A musician is always accepted everywhere. We look at musicians, judge them, and associate with them because of how they sound. I don't care where they are from, or their ethnic background; I am involved with pleasing sounds.

We don't see each other, we hear each other, and it is a wonderful way to approach life.

The word *bass* means *bottom*, the lowest part; it is the foundation of a building. It has to be strong or the edifice will not stand. It's the lowest voice in the human, the lowest stringed instrument, and the lowest sounding instrument section in the orchestra. Like Atlas, I hold the entire band up, and I love it. I am making them sound good. If the song is "Body and Soul," boom (bass) — da-dee-da-dee-da — dee — dee — boom — dee-dee-dee-dee-dee . . . the bass hits first.

Music sustains me and keeps me "physically fit and morally straight." My dream has always been to be a good musician and to be respected among them. Consequently I have been temperate. Anything that's going to deter or keep me from being a proper musician or a good musician, I don't even consider.

I've been married to my wife, Mona, for fifty years. She handles most of the business things and she's a church-going lady. I've been a deacon of my church for five years. That may not be good publicity for a jazz musician, but it is wonderful for me. If somebody gets busted you hear about it immediately, but if you've been married to the same lady, raised a family, and have a great respect for humanity and the world, this doesn't make sensational copy for the tabloids. There are many good musicians who live similar lives.

Milt ("The Judge") Hinton

I think of Shakespeare's words "To thine own self be true." I am always saying to my students and other young people who come to me for advice: "You can tell me anything, but know your weaknesses."

Practicing means working on something that you don't know. You should take it very slowly until you feel comfortable and accelerate to the necessary tempo. That's called "progress," and if you keep playing the same passage over and over again, after you've mastered it, it's called "entertainment."

My teacher told me years ago: "This will be your job for the rest of your life; try to master the challenge because it is going to fight you all the way." The most beautiful music can come to you, but to be able to execute it you need to practice.

I have experienced the inequities of life but music has kept me sane. In *Bass Line,* a book I wrote with the help of a student of mine (and the son I never had), David Berger, I talk about what it was to be a black musician in an era of racism. However, no matter the problems I encountered, I was always determined to pursue my career. For example, I remember playing with Cab Calloway's band; the hall would be jammed with admirers and we would have a bushel basket full of money but when we had finished playing they wouldn't sell us a sandwich, and we had to ride two or three hundred miles before we could get something to eat. I recorded this era of disparity with my camera. I felt the need to preserve the evidence of this prejudice. In my book I have pictures of some great musicians standing under signs that say, "Motel for Colored" and "For Colored Only." Through the years I have taken pictures of the black reality, to show how it was. In one photo of mine of a railroad station in Atlanta, Georgia, in 1939, I immortalized the sign saying "Colored entrance." Now, fifty years later, there is a black mayor who is running for governor of the state. So, times are changing.

My grandmother was born a slave, had thirteen children that she brought up alone, and lived to be one hundred and three. Thanks to her good influence, I am not bitter. She said I should be strong. Her words were: "Don't let anybody tell you that you are inferior; the mere fact that you have survived all this makes you know that you are strong and have an important heritage. You can do anything you want if you set your mind to it" were her words.

My mother was the only child in her family with a chance of an education. They taught her piano and she was one of Nat "King" Cole's teachers. We all grew up in Chicago in a Christian home. I was taught the dignity of the words "Do unto others as you would have them do unto you." Not as they did unto you but as you would like for them to do. I really believe in this.

I am grateful to have lived long enough to see the great progress in our nation. While most immigrants of different nationalities and ethnic origin come here by choice, black people were brought here as slaves. But I have great faith in our young people.

My mother and father separated when I was three months old, and the first time I saw my father I was thirty. We were poor. However, there was always twenty-five cents or fifty cents for a music lesson. My grandmother was completely independent. She said: "Take what you've got and make what you want." We never missed a meal. My family refused welfare; our philosophy was "Earn your money; it is a great reward to want something and work and save for it. Then when you get it, you will cherish it, because you know how many hours it took to obtain that particular thing. Take good care of it and nourish it, because you have earned it rightfully."

I might have been crazy when I was young, but I always knew nothing was going to interfere with my playing.

I look around now and say: "Where is

everybody?" My friends who were heavy smokers and drinkers are no longer here. I too smoked, but when I found out it was not good I stopped. I tell my friends when they come around to "rap" and ask: "Mr. Hinton, can I help you carry your bass?" and I say: "Son, when I get so I can't carry it, then I'll quit playing it." I want to be independent as long as I can.

The only advice is: whatever you want, want it badly enough to do anything to earn and acquire it. If it is an education, you must really want an education. You must want to learn to read books — you can go everyplace in the world through a book. And with music you can do the same thing; you can listen to the music and say, "I would like to play like that" and want it badly enough to work hard enough to emulate what you've heard. It's all a matter of being hungry for something and thinking, "I want to be me; I don't want to be my father's son." There's a niche in the world for everyone.

I work very hard all the time and I also have a senior citizen garden, two blocks from my house. Every morning, if I am in the city, I work in my salad garden. Then I come back to the house and practice for twenty minutes before breakfast. In that way I "earn" the right to eat breakfast. Everything should be earned, and exercise gives you an appetite. It is a matter that nobody's giving you anything. You yourself have earned it.

A typical day for me is recording in the morning and working until midnight in a club. It may be a long day, but I enjoy it and I nonetheless find time to relax. Music is a beautiful world to live and play in.

Horst P. Horst

Born in Germany in 1906, Horst P. Horst first studied art at the Kunst-gewerbeschule in Hamburg and later with Le Corbusier in Paris. He learned the art of photography by assisting Hoyningen-Huene in his Paris studio. In 1932, Mr. Horst was invited to New York to photograph for **Vogue;** *he moved permanently to the United States in 1940 and has worked for Condé Nast Publications ever since. His innovative and elegant work has been exhibited worldwide, as well as in several of his own books, including* **Salute to the Thirties** *and* **The History of Fashion Photography.** *He lives in Oyster Bay, Long Island.*

Thuringia, where I was born, is one of the most beautiful and poetic parts of Germany. Weimar, where I spent a lot of my early youth, had for years been a sort of German cultural capital. . . .

My family was middle-class and relatively prosperous, up to the outbreak of World War I when I was eight years old. But by the end of the war we youngsters didn't have much to eat, so when we got out of school we went into the countryside to pull up weeds and bring them back home, to add to the vegetables from our small garden. That kind of deprivation, I believe, did me no harm in the long run. Children who are brought up too comfortably often end up doing nothing but complaining. I myself have never been satisfied with my work; I am constantly striving to do better.

An aunt of mine had a small summer place, within easy reach of the Bauhaus [founded by Walter Gropius in Weimar]. One of the Bauhaus students who stayed with her there, Eva Weidemann, a dancer, was ten years older than I. She was the love of that part of my life. Through Eva I learned about another world — the world of the mind and the spirit. As a teen-

Horst P. Horst

ager, because of a small spot on my lung, I was sent off to a sanatorium at Leysin in Switzerland. The solitude there forced me to look inward and learn patience. Otherwise, there was only the Dent du Midi to look at, in the distance, and Eva's wonderful weekly letters to sustain me.

After working for an import-export firm in Hamburg, which bored me, I entered the Hamburg School of Applied Art, where Gropius was director, and made furniture. In the end that bored me too, and wanting to seek new horizons I wrote to the architect Le Corbusier in Paris. He wrote back: "You can come anytime; come right away, if you want to study with me." So I went to Paris. Sadly, I found Le Corbusier rather unlikable as a person, and only stayed a short while, working as his apprentice. Paris in the early 1930s was a heady place for a young German, and I was prepared to try anything in the way of a job. I modeled bathing suits — rather shocking for that period, but why not; I had a good body — for the *Vogue* photographer Georges Hoyningen-Huene; and started to work as his assistant. That's the way I first learned about photography, and eventually worked as a photographer at the Vogue studio in Paris myself. To teach myself about lighting and posing and composition, I used to visit the Louvre and study the work of the old masters.

In 1932, Condé Nast, the owner of *Vogue,* invited me to spend six months under contract in New York. I didn't know anyone there and I was very lonely. Mr. Nast was very meticulous as well as a fearful snob. One day he summoned me, and criticized my work: "This flower is out of focus." When I started to defend myself, he got quite angry and said, "I suppose you think you're as good a photographer as Steichen!" I replied that if I didn't hope to be as good as Steichen one day, I might as well not try to be a photographer. "I've never heard such arrogance," Nast replied. "You will leave here as soon as the contract is over." I told him that I was leaving by the next boat. And I did. . . .

So I went back to Paris, and worked for French *Vogue* again. I already loved Paris, and felt at home with the people at the *Vogue* Paris office, as well as made friends with Parisians — who can be marvelously loyal friends, once you learn to speak French and they come to like you. Some of my 1930s acquaintances in France have become legendary figures today: Jean-Michel Frank the designer, Julien Green the American-born writer, now a French Academician, Bébé [Christian] Bérard the painter, Cocteau, Gertrude Stein, Janet Flanner, Charles and Marie-Laure de Noailles, Gide, Dali, and Picasso.

Condé Nast finally changed his mind and asked me to return to New York. Until the outbreak of World War II, I spent half of every year in France and half in America. But Paris was still my real home; and one of my best friends on either side of the Atlantic was a Frenchwoman, Chanel. I had met her by chance at a dinner at the Paris Exhibition in 1937. The next day she called asking me to take her photograph. *Vogue* was excited about that, because for two years Chanel had not allowed the magazine to attend her collections. She arrived, and I took her photograph. When Chanel saw it, she telephoned me to say "It's all right as a photograph of a dress, but it has nothing to do with me." I said: "How could it? I don't even know you!" She agreed, and invited me to dinner. I saw a great deal of her and I took the photographs of her that she liked best — and that are among the works of mine that are still my own favorites. We always had a sort of love affair without . . . as Chanel said: "Everything but exercise . . . no, no exercise!" Every time I went to see her, she gave me presents, mostly furniture, of a kind I'd never pos-

Going Strong

sessed. She furnished my Paris apartment with objects that I later brought back to New York when I had to leave Europe in 1939.

In 1943 I was drafted into the U.S. Army. Learning to be an American soldier when I was still officially considered an enemy alien wasn't easy. My years in the Army were the best time I had in my life.

After the war I went back to work for Condé Nast Publications; and I have continued to do so ever since. . . . Right now I'm preparing two books and working with four galleries in the United States, Europe and Japan. . . . While I don't follow any particular health regime, I don't eat anything fattening. Friendships are important to me. My friends have always given me moral support. It's a good thing to share your life.

The best thing I can say about the lessons I have learned from life is: if you have troubles when you are young, just go your own way if you want to survive. I have had no desire ever to be "against" anything: it's a waste of energy. My ambition was never to make money. My aim has always been to live in a way that stimulates me as well as to give people happiness. I believe in Saint Francis: "Where there is hatred, let me sow love. . . . For it is in giving that we receive." To the young, I would say: "Never stop trying. Keep on learning, always. Keep your eyes open. Try to make great things out of small things."

"Never stop trying. Keep on learning, always."

Mabel James

Mabel James was born in Newport Gwent, South Wales, in 1908. In 1926 she moved to London, where she had a succession of jobs, including working as a housemaid and sausage plaiter. Since 1963, she has worked as the head cloakroom attendant at Annabel's, a London nightclub.

Make up your mind that you're not going to get old. I have. I live every day to the fullest. My parents used to say, "If you can't do a good turn, don't do a bad one."

You've got to overcome adversity. I've got the support of a lovely son. He's made me so happy.

I've worked since I was fourteen. And I got married when I was twenty-three and my husband died eighteen years later. It was a terrible jolt. After your spouse dies you have to pull yourself together. You can't bring him back, and you have to accept that in the end. I didn't get very much money from the government to keep my son and me going. I had to go to work.

I came from Newport Gwent, in South Wales. My first job was in service there. My mother wouldn't let me come to London because in Gwent, they think the worst of it. But when I was eighteen I came to London, and my first job in the city was in Brompton Square working for a lovely lady, Mrs. Arkwright, who really cared about me. If she thought I was a bit fed up and knew I would like to have a dance, she would say to the lady's maid, "Make Mabel a frock and give her a ticket for a dance." Her generosity and thoughtfulness to others was a good example for a young girl. I met my husband at a dance at the Chelsea town hall. "Don't let's quarrel, because I never intend to get married to you," he said. I answered, "You'd be lucky," and walked away. I didn't see him for two years. Then he turned up and asked me to marry him.

For the past twenty-seven years, I've been working at Annabel's nightclub. The owner, Mark Birley, is the greatest. I've been very lucky. I never expected to do this well.

I never get to bed till four in the morning. I get up at noon, do things at home, and then I go to the club about half past six. Once I am there, I make sure everything's clean and fold the towels. The staff has a meal at seven-thirty and then wait for the guests. It gets interesting then. The only thing I ever keep secret is when some of the guests are philandering. They say, "I've got a pink ticket, Mabel." So now I say, "You've got a pink ticket?" And I never tell. Working in clubs or restaurants, you've got to be polite. Actually it doesn't cost anybody anything to be polite. People used to be more elegant. Some of these young girls, they've got lovely legs, but they've got elastic bands around them for skirts. And they can hardly walk. Shame really, because some of them got lovely figures.

I always make a point of going out on my day off for a walk or shopping. The only vitamin I take is Minalka. I've been taking it for seventeen years. I drink scotch but only in moderation. They say it thins the blood.

Every night after work a taxi takes me home. People worry. "Aren't you frightened to go in?" they say. "No, when I get out of the cab, and I go into the door I say, 'Somebody up there loves me.'" And that protects me. The driver waits till I get my key. They're all so good and really look after me. See again, if you're nice to people, they'll be more than helpful back. Just keep the basic values and all goes well.

Earle M. Jorgensen

Chairman of the board and chairman of the executive committee of Jorgensen Steel, Mr. Earle Jorgensen was born in 1899. At the age of fifteen, he left school in order to support his family. At the age of twenty, he began his own scrap iron company. Under his leadership, Jorgensen Steel has expanded to twenty-six plants, employs three thousand people, and does nine hundred million dollars' worth of business per year.

Have courage, confidence, and determination is my motto. I picked it up as a kid along with "Never say die; say damn." I was in my twenties when I started that one. Kipling's poem "If" is one of my great inspirations. When my son was sixteen years old, he wanted me to buy him an automobile. I said, "Look, son, if you memorize Kipling's 'If,' and recite it letter-perfect, I'll go down with you and buy you your first car." About a week later, he came back. He got his car.

Life just goes on for me. I have enjoyed working hard since I started as a very young man. My dad died when I was about thirteen, and when I was fifteen we ran out of money. I had to go to work as an office boy to support my mother in San Francisco; I made twenty-five dollars a month. If my dad hadn't died while I was so young, I probably would have followed his footsteps and gone to sea and retired as a sea captain. But instead I entered the business world.

I remember many trips with my parents. When my father was a sea captain, he was allowed to take his family with him. I remember going around Cape Horn when I was six, in his schooner.

My day starts at five-fifteen A.M., with the exception of Saturdays and Sundays, when I wake up at seven-thirty A.M. I take a half-hour of exercise, have my breakfast, and at seven I leave for the office.

On weekends and holidays I play tennis. I'm a great believer in keeping the mind and body busy. If you do that, you'll achieve a good long life. So many company policies mandate retirement at age sixty-five. My advice is — if you have to retire, go into the outside world and find something else. If you cannot find paid work, there are organizations like the Red Cross and the Cancer Society who need help all the time. Even if you work for free, you will feel as though you are benefiting humanity. Sometimes, the new pursuit becomes more fulfilling.

When I was eighteen I served in World War I driving the first American tanks. At that time there was no draft. Patton was the first lieutenant in my company and Dwight Eisenhower was then lieutenant colonel and head of the first American Tank Corps.

After coming out of the service, I returned to work in San Francisco and started working for a lady who was in the toy and novelties business, importing from Europe. She said if it worked out, she'd give me a quarter of the company. She sent me back to New York to open and keep a small base there to sell Christmas tree ornaments, dolls, and all kinds of imports. But she went broke and I didn't get my paycheck. I walked onto the New York streets with twenty-five cents in my pocket looking for a new job.

A friend of mine had bought lots of scrap

Earle M. Jorgensen

iron, which he shipped to the Orient. He said, "If ever you are in trouble in New York, go see Count Luschinsky; I buy lots of scrap from him." So I did. Luschinsky said: "You are a bright young man. Get yourself out of New York and go back to the West Coast. And work with these junk dealers who are buying up war salvages. Learn something about the business, and I think you'll end up in business for yourself."

I pulled my pockets inside out to show him I had only twenty-five cents, so I couldn't go back to the Coast. He gave me two hundred dollars and said, "You pay me back someday when you can." A few years later, when I had the money to pay him back, I couldn't find him.

That's how I started. I went to work for a firm called Body Industry. They sent me to Los Angeles, but it didn't work out too well and I decided I'd go into business for myself on Third and Spring streets. I was able to rent desk space for fifteen dollars a month, but I was short two dollars. I had two suits, so I went down Spring Street and I pawned one for two dollars and came back and was able to pay the first month's rent.

I worked every night. One evening, a short stocky man stopped me and said, "Hello, son, how are you?"

"I'm fine," I said.

"Do you live here?" he said.

"No, I don't. I'm trying to."

He said, "I'd like to have dinner and talk to you sometime. How about tonight?"

"I can't tonight. I'm going back to write and send my letters."

He said, "How about tomorrow? Meet me at the Union League Club at seven P.M."

Which I did. We had a marvelous dinner — steak, potatoes — and he concluded the evening by saying, "Listen, son, meet me at the bank tomorrow morning. I am going to lend you twenty thousand dollars to help you out."

Total strangers have always helped me in life. I went to the Mare Island Navy Yard because I'd heard they were having a public auction of steel and equipment from World War I. I bought a freight car, some compressors and a couple of air conditioners. I went up to see the chief engineer with some pictures of material I wanted to sell to them. He said, "Son, give me a couple of days and check back."

In three days he said, "You know, son, I can use all your material and I'll give you forty thousand dollars for the whole thing." We shook hands, I thanked him, and left with the forty thousand dollars.

I went one block down the street and rented a room in the Washington Building. I hired a stenographer and restarted this company. I didn't have any inventory. I found these junk dealers who had bought ships that were out of service during the war. I made deals and sold to them. Some paid me commission and some trusted me; I came back and paid them. I made a little money and I bought a little of the salvage myself. There was an outfit in San Francisco that was bringing in imported steel and dumping it on the West Coast market. I asked if they would give some steel on consignment. They said they would but that my credit wasn't any good. A friend wrote a letter guaranteeing my credit and they proceeded to give me a thousand tons on consignment. That was really the beginning of this business.

Bethlehem Steel heard about me; they were just branching out in the alloy business. They thought I would be a good outlet. They made a long-term deal with me. And that's how I really got started with my own inventory. Now I have twenty-four franchised stations from Hawaii to Philadelphia.

I had to quit grammar school in the eighth grade and start work. To get an education, I went to night high school and later night college, taking courses in business administration. I also studied Japanese and German. I received a very good education without ever earning a diploma in my life. Today I am a trustee at Cal Tech and sit among all those guys with Ph.D.'s. I give a lot of scholarships and help young men in college and high school because I firmly believe in education. My advice is: first get a good education. Then go to work and work hard. Enjoy the work you are doing, work long, and don't mind the hours. Your job will become your hobby and pleasure. I worked all my life and I still enjoy working. My wife, once in a while, says, "You ought to slow down a little bit, and you don't have to go to work so early." I reply, "OK, I'll retire," to which she exclaims, "Don't you dare retire. I married for love, not lunch." So, I go back to work.

I have been married to my present wife for thirty-seven years and they have been the happiest years of my life. We've both been married before.

As a young man I didn't have any friends or family who had money. Both of my parents influenced me enormously. The one thing my mother taught me when we were poor was the importance of neatness and cleanliness. I've followed that all through my life. In all my plants, you can eat off the floor. I might have a plant that's not making money, but the plant better still be neat and clean. The greatest advertising in the world is when a customer visits and sees a pristine factory; they trust it to be a good place to do business.

When I was sixteen and an office boy, I picked up a sign reading "Hustle, that's all." I've kept the original pinned on my wall and copies hang in all my offices. "Hustle" keeps you on your toes.

I have always watched my diet, but I'm a great believer in desserts. I go to bed between ten P.M. and midnight.

Giving credit to people under me has always been my practice. I've hired a lot of smart people who have been very loyal to me. The credit goes to my employees.

In the last couple of months there was a buyout. And this company is going to be twice as big. Our sales were five hundred million; now we're going to be nine hundred million a year, and we added another thousand employees. It's still the Earle Jorgensen Company, and they're keeping me on as chairman of the board and of the executive committee. I plan to be working for a while yet.

Minna Keal

The British composer Minna Keal was born in London in 1909. She originally attended the Royal Academy of Music, where she studied composition with William Alwyn and piano with Thomas Knott. While a student there, she was awarded the Elizabeth Stokes Bursary for her compositional abilities.

In 1975, at the age of sixty-six, she resumed her compositional studies with Justin Connolly, with a string quartet of hers premiering in 1979. Since then, she has completed three other works, including her symphony, which had its first public performance at the Royal Albert Hall in London in 1989.

Whatever my circumstances have been, I've always tried to turn them to my best advantage. When I had to give up my music and earn a living I continued to play the piano. While I was working in the fur trade — dull, menial work — I managed to go once a week to the Guildhall School of Music and Drama and take piano lessons. To give myself an incentive, I worked toward an L.R.A.M. teacher's diploma.

You've got to make sure that throughout your life you've used your gifts and interests to the widest possible capacity. When I reached retirement age, I made up my mind that I would live this period as if my whole life was in front of me. Each day is a new day for me and I want to make the most of it. I'm extremely lucky because I am able to fulfill my teenage dreams. I would like to remind people who are retiring they've got a kind of grant, they've got their pension, their barest necessities are provided for. It is therefore the first time in their life that they can discover what they weren't able to accomplish until then and have the opportunity to pursue new goals.

My husband spoils me by bringing me a cup of tea in the morning. I start my work at about ten o'clock. After a break for lunch, I work some more. Two days a week, I teach piano. I stop working at four. I never work in

Minna Keal

the evenings. My husband has been wonderfully supportive, and I could not compose without him.

I enjoy teaching very much, and I feel very involved and committed to my students both professionally and personally. There's still a lot I want to achieve. I could not imagine living without being stretched fully. My first marriage broke down, and until I met my present husband, I was very unhappy. I brought up my son alone. There were thirteen years between the marriages.

Artistic fulfillment is crucial for me. But human relations play an important part in my life as well. One of my happy memories is that during the rise of Hitler my first husband and I managed to get about two hundred children rescued from Nazi Germany and place them in English homes.

I'm a very obstinate person. If I want to do something and if it's humanly possible, I'll do it. I never wasted energy bemoaning my fate. That is nonproductive. I'm anxious that my music should live on.

My mother was quite exceptional in that our house was always filled with all kinds of people who were quite frankly rather mad and she'd take them on their own level as though they were sane. We were brought up in an environment of great hospitality and goodwill. Visitors would arrive at our home and we'd say, "You can stay for the night," and they might stay for six weeks. My mother still lives on in my memories because of her goodness.

I joined the Communist Party in the thirties and left it in 1957 after the Soviet troops invaded Hungary. Until then I believed we were changing the world for the better. It was shattering to me to find out that we'd been doing exactly the opposite.

I suffer from rheumatism and a sort of chronic bronchial condition. In the morning I always do breathing exercises and special exercises for my rheumatism. We thought we couldn't live in the country without a car. It's turned out to be a good decision because we now take walks — going to the post office involves an hour's walking, and that's very healthy for us. I do not take any medications. Exercising is the key.

I went to an absolutely magnificent school — the Clapton Country Secondary School. It had a very avant-garde Fabian Socialist headmistress, Dr. Mary O'Brien Harris. She instilled in us a good sense of values. When I was ten, I composed a little hymn. Everyone made a fuss of it. It is then that I decided that I would like to become a composer. When my father died, instead of going to the university, I helped my mother part-time in the business, a Hebrew bookselling and publishing company. I took music lessons twice a week, with piano as my first subject and composition as my second subject at the Royal Academy of Music. Composing took over. Yet, I didn't foresee it as a profession. The pressure to give it up came more from other people than within myself. I gave it up for forty-six years, being quite sure I would never compose again. I started composing again when I retired.

By the time I retired, at sixty, I had taken a qualification as a piano teacher and a theoretical qualification for harmony and counterpoint. Justin Connolly, an up-and-coming composer, looked at my compositions and encouraged me to start again, in 1975, when I was sixty-six years old. The first three movements of my first symphony were performed at St. John's Smith Square in 1984. The complete symphony (including the fourth movement) was performed at a promenade concert on September 4, 1989. It took me five and a quarter years of hard work to complete. I composed a shorter piece for violin and orchestra. Before the symphony came two shorter pieces. I am currently working on a cello concerto. I'm sure it will take me at least five years, so I must live until I'm about ninety in order to finish it.

For young people who aspire to become composers, my advice is not to allow commercial considerations to distract them from what they really want to do. If they want to compose seriously, while success may not come, it is imperative to persist.

"Each day is a new day for me and I want to make the best of it."

Gene Kelly

The world-renowned dancer, actor, and director Gene Kelly was born on August 23, 1912, in Pittsburgh, Pennsylvania. After graduating from the University of Pittsburgh, Mr. Kelly began his career in show business, starring in such Broadway productions as **Leave It to Me** *(1938),* **Time of Your Life** *(1940),* **One for the Money** *(1939), and* **Pal Joey** *(1941). Mr. Kelly has also starred in the movies* **The Three Musketeers** *(1950),* **An American in Paris** *(1950),* **Singin' in the Rain** *(1951),* **Brigadoon** *(1954),* **Hello, Dolly!** *(1970) and* **That's Entertainment, Part 2** *(1976), among others.*

Mr. Kelly received Kennedy Center Honors in 1982 and the Lifetime Achievement Award from the American Film Institute in 1985.

The inspiration for my choreography often comes to me spontaneously, while I am working. I can't tell you exactly where I get my creative energy and life force. The difficulty in creating anything — I can speak only for dancing — consists in translating what is in your mind, your mental image, and shaping it into a visual, three-dimensional thing that can be called "dancing." This process is especially difficult in film, where you need to tailor the type of dancing so that it not only fits in with the particular picture, but also fits your character and, hopefully, works with the plot. Much of the dancing will evolve out of the script, or be inspired by a song, but a lot of it just comes spontaneously. And then follow the sweat, blood, and tears.

I've always preferred choreographing to the actual performing. I am not an outright performer; in fact, I don't even like it that much. In all of my films, I loved creating the dance, and was less excited to do the performing. But that aspect has to be done, and I always did dance.

As a child I hated dancing. My mother sent my brother and me to dancing school when we were about seven and eight. It was one of those old-time dancing schools, and of course we were considered the sissies on the block. The only thing I did learn from the experience was to be a good street fighter. . . . After a few years of that, our mother finally stopped sending us to dancing school. Then later, in high school, I became interested in dance only because the girls preferred the fellows who could dance. And dance, it seems, grew and grew in me. But, from the professional dancing point of view, I was a late bloomer.

I don't think anyone ever really learns about himself if he's in a creative business because, as a performer, you need to be constantly aware of other people; you are putting out for them. When I do dance with a girl, for example, I believe it's my duty and also the way the film should be (I'm only talking about films with dance numbers) that you direct everything toward the girl, make her look good. If she looks good, the pas de deux looks good. This theory has stood me in good stead, I believe.

I don't like amateurs. When people come

Gene Kelly

in to work and are not really professional, I become very angry. I have learned that about myself. I have often accepted to do certain pictures just for the sake of working with professionals such as Jimmy Stewart, Henry Fonda, Spencer Tracy, and Freddie March. These colleagues not only have natural talent, but also have worked at their particular craft to become the professionals they are.

I can be very mercurial, but also patient with slow learners. When I am directing, I try to keep the cast happy. If I am doing dances, if they have a tough time learning the steps, I can be very encouraging. It is only when they are dogging it that I can become mean.

I had several mentors. Bernice Holmes was one. She was a woman I studied ballet with for a couple of years in Chicago. The fellows who inspired me most when I was in the Broadway theater were John Murray Anderson, from whom I learned so much, and Robert Alton, who not only taught me a great deal about choreography, but encouraged me to reach for my goal, while other people on Broadway thought I was a bit nutty. I worked with George Abbott as a performer in *Pal Joey* and later, as a choreographer as well as stage director for *Best Foot Forward*. Abbott taught me a great deal about timing, and how to relate to actors. He is really a dean in the school of theater and I was fortunate to have been one of his students.

When I was a little boy, I went to see Douglas Fairbanks in a picture, *The Mark of Zorro*. In the very opening of the picture he was practicing with a long whip. A nobleman rode by and Doug accidentally cut off the plume on his helmet. The nobleman rushed in and challenged him to a duel. Fairbanks apologized. All the courtiers who witnessed this were appalled, saying, "How can you apologize when you were challenged to a duel?" Doug's reply was "If you're in the wrong, admit it; if you're in the right, fight." That has remained my

motto throughout my life. So good old Dougie gave this piece of wisdom to me, as a mere nine-year-old.

My daily life has a pleasant pattern. When I get up, I read the paper, go over the mail, and then I sit and think about some of my current projects. For the past couple of years, I have been going on the lecture circuit, and find it very satisfying. America is full of young movie buffs, in colleges and in movie societies, and it is rewarding to see this sustained enthusiasm. Giving lectures has evolved into a real profession for me. Besides, you're paid for it, so it's good all around.

I am currently trying to get some unknown young people together to do a musical. And they're all enthused about it. Whether I can raise the money remains questionable in our present era of the deal. To say, "Here are two unknown performers" doesn't help fund raising today. Of course raising money has always been difficult, but in the studio days, you had a lot of people working with you who had faith in your production. Often the unknown people, such as Leslie Caron or Debbie Reynolds, were taken by the studios that were willing to take a risk. Nowadays it is far more problematic to raise capital.

I am also writing my memoirs, which takes several hours a day. I stop whenever I run out of steam. I do not have a set time; I may go into the afternoon or evening, but usually it's one or the other. I have never kept a health regime. The dancing provided enough exercise for me. Now, I am going downhill physically — gradually — and I don't care.

I think it is important to share your life. But, of course, what is more important, and indeed more difficult, is to find the right person. The one thing in my life that made me extremely happy was having my three children. Each birth was the biggest thrill of my life.

I grew up with four brothers and sisters — we had a great childhood with lots of love. And we were a very orderly group. Not that we didn't fight a lot; we certainly did not live in an aristocratic neighborhood. A tightly knit family and Irish Catholic on both sides, we never thought of disobeying our parents — never thought about the things that I see kids doing and saying all around me today. It was an old-fashioned bringing up. Their wonderful example has always been with me. Both my parents shared equally in influencing me. But my mother took great care to keep my brother and me dancing. In fact, during the Depression, when we were strapped for money, my brother and I knew enough about dancing to open our own dancing school. We made good money.

After I graduated from the University of Pittsburgh, I was supposed to go to law school. But I decided against it. I knew I wanted to keep dancing, or at least teach dance. I was drawn to New York; there was nothing left for me in Pittsburgh.

Everything for me has been happenstance. The good parts have been the luck of the Irish and the bad parts I generally worked out for myself.

I am often asked to counsel aspiring dancers and actors. To them, my advice is: "Whatever you do, be prepared to work." I can only speak for the arts, but I think it applies to all professions. Whatever the job is, work, work, work, work and learn every aspect of your trade.

I think the first thing you can do for yourself in life is keep from being bored. If you have exciting work, that's the best defense. My last words are "Love thy neighbor."

Eleanor Lambert

A public relations executive, fashion authority, and journalist, Eleanor Lambert was born in Crawfordsville, Indiana, in 1903. After moving to New York, she became a pioneer publicist for American artists and art works. She also served as a producer for large fashion shows. In 1963, Eleanor Lambert helped to found the Council of Fashion Designers of America. Later she masterminded the National Fashion Press weeks and the International Best Dressed Poll. She is president of her own public relations firm, Eleanor Lambert Limited, and writes a syndicated column concerning women's issues for She *and* World of Fashion.

I'm a good entrepreneur, less good at delegating. I am fortunate in having a very good memory, which enables me to do more than one thing at a time.

I run a publicity office, and my clients are mostly in the fashion and luxury field. One of my English clients is the Hartnell Company. After Norman Hartnell died, his company fell into trouble. Two hours before the bankruptcy announcement, Manny Silverman, the head of Moss Brothers in London, along with another financier and developer, came to the rescue. I have been working for them and enjoy trying to develop the company. It seems to be well on its way, as Marc Bohan is the fashion designer and director. The first collection was a smash hit.

My father left my mother when I was three months old. He was the agent for Ringling Brothers Circus. He was a hardworking man, and despite his absence, his work habits must have influenced me.

I went to art school with the hope of becoming a sculptor. But I soon realized I'd be mediocre and gave that up.

My very happy marriage marked my life. After my husband died, I was in such despair I sought the help of a psychiatrist. "There is a difference between sorrow and mourning," he told me. "You are doing both. You are mourning. And you're going to destroy yourself."

"You have just solved the whole thing for me," I replied. And I never went back.

If you have once been deeply in love with someone, you never lose him or her. You can invoke that person's presence by just thinking about him. Don't waste time on people you don't want to see. But don't forget friends and don't lose them.

When I attended the Chicago Art Institute, we often went to the stockyards for steaks. There were a lot of gypsies that hung around in the old warehouses, and one of them read my palm. "You're never going to be rich, but you'll always have nice things," she said to me. She seemed to have predicted my future.

Valentine Lawford

Valentine Lawford was born in 1911 in Hertfordshire, England. In addition to studying at Cambridge University, Mr. Lawford studied at the University of Strasbourg and the Sorbonne, and in Vienna.

As their respective private secretary, Mr. Lawford served three consecutive British Secretaries of State during the 1930s and 1940s and acted as Winston Churchill's French interpreter whenever the Prime Minister met with de Gaulle. Mr. Lawford also served as the chargé d'affaires at the British Embassy in Tehran, Iran.

After concluding his career with the British Foreign Service in 1950, Mr. Lawford moved to the United States. He is the author of several books, including **Horst P. Horst: His Works and His World** *(1984) and* **Bound for Diplomacy** *(1963). He has also contributed to such publications as* **The Atlantic Monthly** *and* **Esquire**. *Mr. Lawford has also had many showings of his watercolor paintings.*

I was a very shy, frightened little English boy, totally unlike my two elder brothers, who went into the Navy, as my father had done before them. My youngest brother was a good athlete, and is now a landowner and farmer. . . . I was always drawing, painting, playing the piano and the violin, but no one in the family was interested in my efforts, except my mother. She was an artist herself, but she was also a very practical woman, who made me and my brothers and sister work in the garden. I rather think she really preferred women to men, but she and I were exceptionally close to each other. It was from her that I inherited not only my artistic bent but a healthy passion for animals, especially dogs and horses. It was she who taught me to draw and paint and play the piano, from the age of four. She was the guiding influence of my life in childhood and ever after. I was desperately fond of her when I was a boy, and loathed having to leave her for boarding school, at the age of eight. But I managed to get through ordinary private and public school existence quite happily. I never really belonged to any group, at either of my two schools. But my

Valentine Lawford

contemporaries didn't seem to resent that. After I wrote my first book, a partial autobiography entitled *Bound for Diplomacy*, published in 1963, my one-time Repton headmaster, Geoffrey Fisher, the Archbishop of Canterbury, wrote me a letter in which he said that what he most remembered about me as a schoolboy was that I had seemed totally detached from the life of my fellows. (No doubt he was right. But the fact is that privately I was an incurable romantic: from the age of eleven, I have never ceased to be in love with somebody.)

I realize that I have led a very privileged life. But nothing in my life was planned — by me, at least. At twenty-three, I got into the Diplomatic Service and stayed the course for sixteen years. I became private secretary to three British Secretaries of State in World War II, and attended most of the wartime conferences. In 1946 I came to the U.S. as alternate U.K. delegate to the United Nations, and often had to make speeches in debates with the Soviet Union delegates, Gromyko and Vyshinsky. But my heart wasn't in it. At a Russian Easter party in New York in 1947, I met Horst, the famous photographer. From then on, I spent my spare time with him: weekends at his newly built house on Long Island, and weekdays in my apartment at the Plaza Hotel — for which I paid the then phenomenally extravagant daily rate of fourteen dollars. . . .

In the autumn of 1950, after a stint as chargé d'affaires at the British Embassy in Tehran, I resigned from the Diplomatic Service and came back to Horst's house to live, and take my chance as a free-lance. My decision to change horses in midstream, at the age of thirty-nine, wasn't an easy one. I had no wish to offend my colleagues, or my parents. But it turned out quite well, in the event. My former friends in the F.O. [Foreign Office] remained friends —

they had so many more important things to worry about. My mother, naturally, acquiesced. Best of all surprises: my father acquiesced too, in the course of time.

As a child I had felt rather distant from him. His naval duties often took him away from home. He was a conventional disciplinarian of the old school, and frankly found me puzzling. He was proud of me when I gained scholarships, of course, and even prouder when I passed into the Diplomatic Service. It had been partly because of his own First World War experience of the Foreign Office — as liaison officer between the F.O. and the Ministry of Blockade — that he had first had the idea that I might fit into the Diplomatic Service, which according to him had been full of eccentric characters, barely capable of surviving in an unsheltered world. . . . For years, I didn't let him meet Horst. But when they finally met, my father's only comment was "Why the hell didn't you introduce me to that nice fellow before?"

By now, Horst and I have known each other for forty-three years, and we have lived and worked together, producing articles and books. It isn't easy, though, to work in harness with a genius. And in the 1970s I gradually forsook writing for painting. In contrast to writing, which I found increasingly difficult — no wonder that many writers are driven to drink! — I have found painting — first landscapes, and for the last decade almost exclusively flowers — an irresistible sensual pleasure and an endless source of happiness and satisfaction. The subject of *retiring* has never entered my mind. I think retiring is almost like saying you want to die. One has to be prepared to die, but I don't want death to come any earlier than it must, so long as I am feeling as healthy and well as I do. The secret of happiness is work, and the greatest good fortune is when your work is something you

Going Strong

love doing. In childhood I dreamed of being a musician, a poet, a painter, a sculptor, a steeplechase rider, and a mountaineer, all at once. Until a few years ago, I climbed in the Austrian Alps like a goat. But now I know better, and am content to stay put, and sit most of the day in my room looking out at the garden and painting flowers. I used to paint in oils, but today my medium is watercolor. It strikes me as a little less pretentious. And, amazingly, I have little difficulty in selling almost every watercolor I can produce . . . either to private collectors in Europe and America, or to Tiffany and Company in New York. . . .

In difficult moments, I still have an old-fashioned way of saying to myself, "Rise above it." And it always works. I'm a reluctant heathen, but I'm a convinced believer in the efficacy of prayer. I still hold imaginary conversations with my mother (who died in 1964) and regularly follow her imaginary advice. No doubt she is responsible for the fact that at all times I have a funny kind of inner strength and confidence. For me, growing old is not such a horrible experience. Every decade of my life so far has been better than the last.

Probably I've been much too frank in what I've told you. But that has always been my way. I have never been able to distinguish between the so-called serious and the so-called frivolous. No wonder I decided forty years ago that I wasn't cut out to be a diplomatist.

"The greatest good fortune is when your work is something you love doing."

Irving Lazar

The artist's representative and lawyer Irving Lazar was born in Stamford, Connecticut, on March 28, 1907. He started practicing law in New York City in 1931, and became an artist's agent in 1933. In 1936, he went to work as an agent for the Music Corporation of America and stayed until 1942, when he joined the Army Air Force. Mr. Lazar operates his own agency, representing authors, often selling the television and film rights of their books. Long considered one of the top agencies in the entertainment business, the Irving Paul Lazar Literary Agency has offices in Beverly Hills and New York.

I inherited my genes from a father who was a fine entrepreneur and who had a lot of energy and guts. He moved on to many different enterprises with a great deal of skill and courage. You are either a mover and shaker or you're not. If you have a sense of lassitude and can't get yourself motivated, then it's just the way you are.

One of the important factors in longevity is that you take care of yourself, not in a terribly circumscribed way, but quite normally — eat the proper foods, have a reasonable amount of daily exercise — either swim, jog, or walk for at least forty-five minutes. If I'm busy during the entire day, I do forty minutes on a very special stationary bicycle, which engages the movement of your legs and arms simultaneously and gives you essential aerobic exercise.

Another great contribution to my longevity is the fact that I've never accepted an associ-ation which would have required account-ability on my part to anybody. I want to be my own man, and I've stayed that way all my life.

On several occasions I was offered the opportunity to join a group of important associations; to run a studio or to own and manage a large agency which was recognized world-wide. In spite of the fact that the money offered was tempting, I've always refused, because it would have been a matter of my having to submit to becoming accountable.

I've learned to pay close attention to what I like and what I don't like. I avoid situations or people I find boring (which is the greatest crime of all). Also, I'd rather keep away from personal confrontations. That means staying away from people and places that might cause me annoyance or pain or make me disagreea-ble. On the business front, however, I welcome

DECORATION
Forever Picasso
Goodbye Picasso
SOTHEBY'S
HELMUT NEWTON

Irving Lazar

and even enjoy confrontation. As an agent I feel that every day is New Year's Eve for me. I wallow in the fun of being involved in constant battles with publishers, studios, and producers. They are my enemy and I beat them at their own game — most of the time.

I don't like getting up early in the morning. I never did. I went through law school and Fordham University at night. I don't usually take any calls before ten A.M. I don't see why anybody has to do anything before that time. As long as I've lived, I've never gotten into contact with the day's work until about ten A.M. I don't mind working on Saturdays, Sundays, or Christmas Day, but I like to sleep in the morning — the civilized way.

I observe no particular religion. My religion is simply to try to be a decent, honest fellow and treat people with courtesy.

One of the most important qualities is to have a goal; decide what you want to do as early in life as you can. Try to accomplish that goal and it will bring you the greatest amount of satisfaction. You have to set a standard of life-style, a standard of the type of people you want to be associated with, and, combined with your work, this will give you a worthwhile life. So you have your work, your exercise, and of course, girls' legs. It is very important that you are in a constant state of observation and evaluation. Unless you become very expert at this, you're missing a lot of fun.

One of the most rewarding factors in my life has been that I've friends everywhere. From Taipan to Europe to Oakland, California, and they're waiting for me whenever I get there, as I'm always waiting for them when I'm in New York or California. Seeing my friends throughout my travels has really been the fabric of my life.

I didn't marry until I was fifty-five years of age and was lucky to find just the right person in Mary. We have complementary tastes and it's worked very well.

Going Strong

"As an agent, I feel that every day is New Year's Eve for me. I wallow in the fun of being involved in constant battles with publishers, studios, and producers."

Leo Lerman

Leo Lerman was born on May 23, 1914, in New York City. Mr. Lerman attended the Fagin School of Dramatic Art in the year 1933–1934. He had a many-faceted career in the theater before exchanging it for a literary one. In 1948, he became a contributing features editor for **Mademoiselle,** *a position he held until 1971. Later, he was the features editor at* **Vogue** *and the editor-in-chief at* **Vanity Fair.** *Currently, Mr. Lerman is the editorial adviser to Condé Nast Publications. Mr. Lerman's several books include* **Leonardo da Vinci: Artist and Scientist** *and the Lotus Club Award–winning* **Museum: 100 Years of the Metropolitan Museum of Art.**

I think every single day is a surprise. There are certain moments when you could possibly feel your age but a great joy can outwit it. I am in the process of outwitting it.

I've always felt everything was possible. I don't want to go to the moon. I'd be delighted to discover there were creatures on another planet, but I don't really want to go there. It's fantastic enough to go to Los Angeles or Miami.

I grew up in a large family of cousins and uncles and aunts, some considered very beautiful. I never was, so I learned early I would have to be funny to be noticed. I was raised until I was thirteen in a deeply Orthodox Jewish, united family; we either laughed or fought a great deal.

Despite the fact that for a great part of my life I never had much money, I always managed to acquire beautiful objects. The rule always was: don't buy something you can't afford, but always spend a little more if you feel that you simply have to have it. I hate owing money. I never lend anything to anybody. I'd rather give.

I don't have a particular health regime, but I do take vitamins.

Being superstitious has helped me get through life.

What makes me happy? To write.

I was raised speaking Yiddish and learned English as a second language. When I was about seven I won a purple pencil at school for writing a perfect English sentence. I've worked in department stores, been a designer, a stage manager, and even a very bad actor — but a great part of my life was spent being a writer.

The best advice I can give to an aspiring writer is, work with somebody who really knows what he or she is doing. And listen carefully. Then sit and write and write and write. Never be afraid of taking risks. Accept the fact that you might possibly not be Marcel Proust. Write every day.

Edna Lewis

The chef and cookbook author Edna Lewis was born in 1914 and grew up in rural Virginia. In 1948, she began cooking professionally and is currently the head chef at Gage and Tollner in Brooklyn, New York. She has written three best-selling cookbooks: **In Pursuit of Flavor** *(1988),* **The Taste of Country Cooking** *(1976), and, with Evangeline Peterson,* **The Edna Lewis Cookbook** *(1983).*

I'm an African American. My grandfather died when I was seven, but somehow I remember him real well. We had a big fireplace and we used to sit and talk about what happened to him when they were slaves. It always made me sad. In other slave societies they'd sometimes keep families and groups together, but here in America, they'd sell off the children. I can't imagine what a mother must have felt when the white owner came one day announcing that the children had to go. It's like children today who are kidnapped and never seen again. Every day my grandfather would wake up with a decision to live the day with dignity, to rise above the daily humiliation. Each day he would renew that resolution. He was strong and decided that once he was free, the first thing he would do was organize a school for his children and neighbors so they could learn to read and write. That was great coming from someone who couldn't do either.

I grew up in a little settlement. Everyone could speak to you and correct you, so all my neighbors and relatives, not just my parents, had a hand in my upbringing. There was something in all of them that I admired. They had

Edna Lewis

certain codes. For instance, your age meant a lot. If you were a certain age, you could do things that a younger person couldn't do. There was an older lady who smoked a pipe with the men. A younger woman could not do that. Once you reached a certain age, you were equal to men and got respect.

I'm sure the Africans discovered cooking meat by fire because they had this kind of combustion that makes fire and they decided to cook it. Sometimes I wonder how people did come to put all these different foods together. How did they decide that egg white was great?

My day starts at five-thirty or six A.M. I come to the restaurant at eight A.M. In the summer, I go to the green market to purchase fresh tomatoes, lettuce, berries, and fruit. When we started out, there were only a couple of organic growers, but now they are multiplying. The cooks we hire know my feelings about food. I try to buy food with the best taste and without additives. While buying the freshest and the best is important, one must look especially for produce with the most taste. The freshest doesn't always necessarily have the best flavor.

I grew up in the country where they didn't spray food or use fertilizer. After I left home, food didn't taste as good as when I was growing up. The *New York Times* recently said the same thing on the front page.

Eating good food is the key to good health. The other day I ate something that was perfectly clean, but it didn't agree with me. I attribute my ill feeling to the fact that I didn't like it. Following your instincts about food is important.

I'm happy to finally be recognized as a cook. I didn't decide to become a chef. All of a sudden, I was consecrated a chef. When I first came to New York, I belonged to a nice group of young people. We used to visit each other frequently. We spent weekends together, and one weekend someone would cook and the next someone else would cook. In the course of one of these weekends one of the men guests announced that he was going to open a restaurant. Turning to me, he said: "You're going to be the cook of my restaurant." That's how it all started and it soon was a big success.

I've written three cookbooks: *The Taste of Country Cooking, In Pursuit of Flavor,* and *The Edna Lewis Cookbook.* And I'm working on my fourth. I never think about retiring, or too much about myself. I guess if you're in good health you just keep on going as long as you can. I used to take a lot of vitamins. Today I only take vitamin C every day.

My advice to young people who want to become chefs is to first learn how food is grown. Young aspiring chefs today should go to work on an organic farm in order to appreciate food. I object to buying something that has no form or shape, like a chicken breast. A lot of young people come out of school with the goal of getting married, investing in a house, and making a lot of money. That's never been a concern of mine.

Until recently, people haven't really paid too much attention to American food. The South has the greatest range of regional cooking in America. I told a young chef from Atlanta who was visiting me and was seeking my advice that he should go back home and research the food and culture of the South because that's where it all started, in all those great plantation houses. Only after fully possessing a grasp of American cuisine should he go abroad to further his knowledge.

I enjoyed being married, but now that I'm alone I enjoy being able to do what I please. I can come and go and I'm not tied to some person that I have to pay attention to. I appreciate being able to do what I want when I want and not having to account to anyone.

I believe in helping others. I also try to

change, with whatever means I have, the system if I feel strongly that certain aspects need improvement. As I was watching some parents the other day with their children, I started thinking how hard it is to guide children today. You have to chart a course for yourself and stick to it. When life is giving you a hard time, you must keep going. There are ups and downs, but you have to surmount those.

Prejudice is still very deep in America; it will always be a racist society. I hoped, back in the sixties, that the young generation of whites would grow up to be different and better than their parents. But that did not happen. Today, there are still a great many people out there who are prejudiced. They can't help it. We just have to exist in this society until maybe it becomes better one day.

"I hoped, back in the sixties, that the young generation of whites would grow up to be different and better than their parents. But that did not happen."

Bella Lewitzky

The internationally known choreographer and dancer Bella Lewitzky was born in Los Angeles on January 13, 1916. After studying at several studios in California, she was the cofounder and codirector of the Dance Theater of Los Angeles from 1946 to 1950, the founder and director of the Dance Associates of Los Angeles from 1951 to 1955, the chairman of the Contemporary Dance Department at the University of Southern California, Idyllwild, from 1956 to 1972, the founder and dean of the School of Dance at the California Institute of the Arts from 1969 to 1972. In 1966, she founded the Lewitzky Dance Company of Los Angeles, which still performs today.

Bella Lewitzky also served as the vice-chairwoman for the Dance Advisory Council to the National Endowment for the Arts from 1974 to 1977 and has also been a committee member of the American chapter of the International Dance Council of UNESCO since 1974.

She has won several awards, including in 1978 **Dance** *magazine's Annual Award and in 1989 the California Governor's Award for Lifetime Achievement in the Performing Arts.*

Going strong, for me, means loving my dance form, my family, and life. When I am involved in a bad situation, I work my way through it, so that it doesn't live inside me. There are techniques to do that. My interest has never been directly in myself, but instead in other people and in the art I've been fortunate to practice.

One should learn to live life for what it offers each day rather than establish closed ex-

Bella Lewitzky

pectations and become so overly preoccupied with details and set formulas. Living is exciting and it shouldn't have time limitations. I think this is true even when the body begins to decay.

Dance has been the single interest of my life. Despite financial concerns, it has been a very fulfilling career. One day I will probably stop. But for the moment, I have no interest in retirement. There are perhaps three or four performances in my life that I remember as nearly perfect. When the performance is exactly as you want it to be, it is as if you are removed from yourself, and able to make comments on your performance, able to observe yourself. I cherish these memories. They have a special niche in my life.

The most traumatic situation I have lived through was when I was called before one of the McCarthy investigative committees. The most un-American thing of all was that committee. And time proved it to be.

My father was a guiding light in my life. He was a gentle, talented man. He was a friend as well as my parent. The love of art was his gift to me.

My working day has changed as I've reached an older age. I'm an early riser. I get up somewhere between five-thirty and six every morning. And I enjoy that solitude. It's too early for people to phone. There are no interruptions even outside — the landscape has not stirred yet. That's when I exercise for about an hour and a half. If I'm working on a new piece, I will go into the studio and begin to sketch what the new piece is. The company arrives at about ten. Classes begin at ten-thirty and run until noon. Rehearsals and choreographic periods from twelve to four-thirty, and after that I usually devote time to administrative work for the company.

I am also working on the "Dance Gallery."

This is a facility meant to have a thousand seats. It will be an experimental, nonproscenium space where dancers who don't wish to embroil themselves in having to attract an audience of proper size or bother with all the lights, costumes, and so on can test their work. This will be a place for both the experimental piece from a very advanced choreographer or something brand new from a young choreographer; it will be a wonderful showcase experimenting arena. Presently, we are trying to raise the capital to get the building up.

For young dancers, a word of advice: Don't enter the world of dance unless you are really possessed with that art form, and unless you can pick yourself up after you've fallen down. Probably the hardest piece of advice and one of the most crucial is: You must be self-reliant and independent.

Three is a very good age to start dancing. A young child's foot should not be confined in a shoe, because the foot is growing, the bones are soft. It needs expansibility, freedom. Strictly ballet — meaning the five positions that form its base, and certain connections of arm and leg that form the base — is too restrictive for a three-year-old. I think a three-year-old needs to learn improvisationally the freedom of motion, which is natural to a child. And if that happens, then she can never be locked up again. However, if children start with a very prescribed form dance, such as, for instance, Spanish dance, their capacity to move forward choreographically or improvisationally is not as great.

My advice to a parent is to find a school of motion where freedom is at the center. Guided freedom. And then at about eight years of age ballet becomes very useful. They're ready then to take more ritualized motion.

I don't take any caffeine, alcohol, excessive

salt or sugar, fats, or red meats. I try to eat as many unpolluted foods as I can. I've been on this particular regime for a long time, and once when I returned to eat a piece of meat, it tasted of chemicals and I imagine it was.

The body is a machine that has irreplaceable parts. As you arrive at my age, you value the capacity to move and you treasure a lot more of what you have left than you did when you were young.

"Living is exciting and it shouldn't have time limitations."

Elizabeth, Countess of Longford

Elizabeth, Countess of Longford, was born on August 30, 1906. In 1929, she became a university extension lecturer for the Workers' Education Association. She signed her first books as Elizabeth Pakenham in the 1950s: **Points for Parents** *(1956),* **Catholic Approaches** *(1959), and* **Jameson's Raid** *(1960). As Elizabeth Longford, she has written such award-winning biographies as* **Victoria, R.I.** *(1964 winner of the James Tait Black Memorial Prize, Nonfiction),* **Wellington: Years of the Sword** *(1969 Yorkshire Post Prize),* **The Queen Mother** *(1981),* **Eminent Victorian Women** *(1981), and* **Elizabeth Rex** *(1983).*

As one gets really old, as I am, goals have to be changed, to a point. I don't believe anyone should ever deliberately say, "I am too old for X." It is important to maintain all one's activities, regardless of one's age. Some things will be impossible to do: for instance, years ago, I used to play tennis. Now I could no more run across a tennis court. However, as long as you find yourself trying to do something, go on.

When I was eighty, I wrote a memoir called *The Pebble Shore* (the title is from Shakespeare's sonnet). I didn't think I'd really remember any-thing. However, the minute I began to recall, memories came flooding back — perhaps far too fast and far too frequently. I did discover things about myself. Whether I made up any as I went along, I am not sure.

I wrote two books before I was sixty, but I wrote most of my books after I turned sixty. I have written nineteen books, some more weighty than others. I never feel happy if I am not working on a new book, and I am just finishing one now. When I began writing, I liked to undertake biographies with immense research; each work would take at least four

Elizabeth, Countess of Longford

years. For a really big one, like *Wellington*, the research took eight years. I no longer take on such commitments because I don't want to have done all the research and then not be able to write the book. I would be sorry to put Antonia, my daughter, or my son, Thomas, in the situation of having to finish my work. So I am doing shorter books; these I can be fairly sure of finishing. Certain types of research call for a great deal of travel, often abroad. These days, most of the manuscript papers seem to be in America. Due to a very serious operation I had two years ago, I am not able to undertake a project that would entail traveling as far as America.

Various recent illnesses dictate my new health regime: no animal fats at all, nor any fatty meat or fish. I drink only skim milk. I'd be very upset to look out my window and no longer see the cattle and the sheep grazing in the lovely field. I don't want to eat them. I take one multivitamin pill a day, plus an additional B or E tablet. The operation I underwent cut all the nerves in my back, and sapped my strength away, but I have willed myself back to recovery. I'm gradually getting better, yet the surgeon told me that some people don't get their balance back for eleven years — so I will have to live a good long time. A year ago, I was hobbling about on two surgical crutches. Now I can walk with a cane, and when I garden, I can dig and hoe. In light of so many dreadful experiences other people have, and the suffering that they manage to endure and overcome, mine was very small.

I am not an introspective person; Frank, my husband, is much more so. I've never gone to a psychiatrist. Perhaps I ought to have, but I would be overcome with sheer boredom.

There are many different sides to my life, such as writing and bringing up a family. The birth of each of my children has given me the most happiness in life. What an extraordinary feeling it is when you are first given a new baby! Almost as wonderful a feeling was the discovery that I was pregnant. I've been pregnant ten times. Raising children is exhilarating and tense, but anything to do with children is complete joy. When writing comes with full force and energizing momentum, that too is a magnificent feeling.

Frank and I have been married for fifty-nine years and have been completely happy. Frank and I usually wake up about seven and I get breakfast. I hope to start work at about half past nine. I give a lot of lectures, which require extensive preparation. I stop work for lunch and have a very spare meal. If I am alone, I sit on the balcony with a tray and read. Afterwards, I usually do my shopping in the early afternoon, and walk around Chelsea or the Physic Garden. In the evening, if we aren't going out, I cook an extremely simple dinner. Then Frank and I listen to the news, and watch whatever is interesting on television. We particularly enjoy when Harold Pinter, my son-in-law, has a play like *The Heat of the Day* showing.

The one thing in my life I have not revealed about myself has to do with my intellectual pride. When I was young everything depended on getting a good degree. Today, I think people don't go by those things quite so much. I hope not, anyway. Word got around that I had been awarded a First Class Honours degree when in fact I hadn't. I had merely received a very good Second. This false information, however, would appear now and then in the press, and each time it did, it gave me tremendous pleasure. I, in fact, almost began to believe the press myself. But I have to contradict it now and admit the truth.

We used to laugh at my father, who was always telling us to be moderate. And if we suggested having a third helping at lunch, he would pompously say, "Moderation in all things!" But funnily enough, I still have that feeling about life — that one should always try and keep a happy medium. And all those boring proverbs about moderation and the Golden Mean, although I used to think them unattractive, have proven to be right for me.

For those writers who are thinking of becoming biographers, I suggest that they first find the right subject. To me, this is the most important. Once you have something that you can understand, that appeals to you, there will inevitably be a certain amount of detective work to do. However, if you are inspired by your subject, in turn you will learn much while writing. It doesn't matter whether the subject is big or little. It has to be something about which you feel passion, something that fuels your imagination.

"I never feel happy if I am not working on a new book."

Dr. Michael McCready

Dr. Michael McCready, born in 1913, is a physician who specializes in the practice of homeopathy, osteopathy, and radionics. During World War II, he was parachuted into occupied France to assist the French Maquis. In addition, he was a member of the British Olympic fencing team. In 1975, Dr. McCready moved from London to Dublin, where he maintains a thriving practice.

I've learned a lot about myself since I became interested in the teachings of Gurdjieff and Ouspensky. Their philosophy is a very ancient one. One of the things they've tried to teach you is to observe yourself, not an easy thing to do. It's much simpler to observe others. You can do so for short times — half a minute or so. I have found this practice very instructive. I think I'm fairly critical about my own activities. Amongst other things, I've learned that I am more prone to worrying than I realized.

Gurdjieff was a remarkable man. He learned a lot by traveling in the Far East. This ancient teaching already known in the civilization that preceded Egyptian civilization actually relates very closely to the teaching of Christ.

Ouspensky believed in practicing conscious love and thought that the best way was to begin by practicing on your dog. I have done that on mine, trying very hard to help my dog live life peacefully and happily. I feel that I have become more in tune with him, and I am quite good at knowing or predicting what he wants. Dogs, in fact, are quite communicative.

Sometime after the war I became interested in Radionics. In the Army, a medical officer had aroused my curiosity. His father was working in Radionics and dowsing and he introduced me to the first American osteopath, in London. I met her and watched her working and was very impressed. The two doctors had a clinic and were taking on a small number of

qualified doctors to teach them osteopathy. I joined the clinic and studied homeopathy and started to study osteopathy, and I found these two fields a very good combination.

Radionics is an unorthodox method of healing at a distance through the medium of an instrument using the ESP faculty. A trained practitioner can then discover the cause of disease within any living system. Suitable therapeutic energies can then be made available to the patient to help restore optimum health. Radionics was originated by a distinguished American physician, Dr. Albert Abrams (1863–1924) of San Francisco, and it has been developed by numerous other research workers. Basic to its theory and practice is the concept that humans and all life forms share common ground in that they are submerged in the electromagnetic energy field of the earth, and that each life form has its own electromagnetic field. If the field is sufficiently distorted, it will ultimately result in disease of the organism. Accepting that "all is energy," Radionics sees organs, diseases, and remedies as having their own particular frequency or vibration.

My day starts at about seven A.M. If I'm doing broadcast treatment and have any urgent cases, I may set two or three cases on the Radionic machine and I change them sometimes every two or three hours. I usually start seeing patients at about half past ten. I treat many of the patients osteopathically, and I see them at about three-quarters of an hour intervals. As I

Dr. Michael McCready

have breaks during the day, I can go on until quite late. I reset some of the machines again at eleven P.M.

There's only a small group of people who are doing this sort of Radionic work, and we keep in touch.

Some time ago, I studied how to use a pendulum and find that research has been very helpful. It's quite a difficult practice to learn to do. It involves tuning in on some other part of the brain to extract information of an intuitive kind. You're really working in a different dimension, because there are problems that can't be worked out by the ordinary brain. If you work with the pendulum, you can very often reach the answer to questions, and that's made my work much more interesting. It's what we call "medical dowsing."

Being a doctor is more of a vocation, not a nine-to-five job. You get to know people and their problems. With many, you become a friend as well as a doctor. If they ring up, you have this obligation to do something about it. I was talking to an old patient, a slightly cantankerous character, and he said, "You know, you've been a very good friend, and I can't tell you how grateful I am." I felt that was quite an accolade.

I am fairly sympathetic about other people's problems. A few months ago, when I was talking to a patient for the first time, she suddenly said, "You're the first doctor who's ever actually listened to me."

I had my orthodox medical training to deal with orthodox problems, but quite often for certain conditions the orthodox treatment is not satisfactory. Then I may give them homeopathic treatment. Practicing and knowing both disciplines gives me a much wider scope. Understanding something about these other "unorthodox" methods of treatment, I can often work out an effective treatment for many more ailments. Homeopaths have some very good treatments for migraine headaches. Combined with careful advice about diet, you can get very good results. A local doctor had told a patient, "Quite frankly, aching backs and medicine are a gray area. You've got to learn to live with it." But with this extra knowledge you can work out toward a cure. A young woman who had been in a motor car accident two years ago suffered pain with her hip ever since — the tests and investigations showed nothing. Doctors deduced that her problem was psychological. They sent her to a psychiatrist. She finally came here. Examining her from an osteopathic point of view, I found that one of the bones in her lower back was out of position. I was able to correct its position.

It's important to pay attention to one's diet; I always ask patients what they're eating or drinking. Migraine headaches are often due to a liver problem; therefore one must stay away from very rich foods.

I think everyone ought to do some exercise every day. Research shows that if people only take a small amount of regular exercise, they're much less inclined to get heart disease.

I have certainly enjoyed my family life, and having children gave me enormous pleasure. My wife has been a tremendous support. We have so much in common. She's also a doctor.

During the war I always took homeopathic remedies wherever I went without advertising the fact. My treatments might not have been approved by the senior medical people in the Army. Nor did I tell the soldiers that they were having anything unusual; it just made the treatment more interesting because there'd be no so-called placebo effect. I hid it from people. When I got good results, as I did quite often there, I knew it wasn't just boosting the hope of the patients.

My brother had very bad asthma. He spent four months of the year in bed. A French dietician and a Genovese homeopathic doctor were the only people who really helped him. My brother started to make tremendous progress. When I became a medical student, I would occasionally ask my teachers, "What is this thing — homeopathy?" "Absolute nonsense" was always the answer. With all these doctors practicing homeopathy, how could it be nonsense? I established the fact that homeopathy sometimes produced very good results.

Going into medicine is a lot of work, and there are many faster ways of making money. Young doctors often work eighty hours a week. You've got to like people and be prepared to try to understand their problems, and be sympathetic. When I was a child, I was rather frightened of doctors, so I was determined I would try very hard to stop people from being afraid of me.

"Being a doctor is more of a vocation, not a nine-to-five job."

Dr. Mildred E. Mathias

Professor Emerita of botany at the University of California, Los Angeles, Mildred E. Mathias was born in Sappington, Missouri, on September 19, 1906. Dr. Mathias earned all of her academic degrees at Washington University, St. Louis, receiving her Ph.D. in 1929. She has been with the U.C.L.A. Department of Botany since 1947.

Dr. Mathias has published some two hundred books and articles, leads natural history tours all over the world, and is a member of numerous professional organizations. The Mildred E. Mathias Botanical Garden at U.C.L.A. is dedicated to her.

No working day is like any other. I teach a very lively awareness class on economic, political, and cultural problems in conserving biodiversity. I want the students to understand what's going on when they read the newspapers and when they see legislation, so they will know how to vote. I also take groups on trips to different places throughout the world on natural history courses that emphasize conservation. We've been to China and the Amazon. The groups consist of a wide variety of people. A recent trip to Africa included a wonderful eighty-five-year-old woman. We went to see a fantastic ruin, Great Zimbabwe, comparable to Machu Picchu, then to Kyle National Park, an animal reserve. After that we traveled on to the Eastern Highlands, where we roamed around the lake area and the national park and later visited the botanical gardens in the highlands. Then we flew to Bumi Hills on Lake Kariba, a safari lodge where there are marvelous cottages cantilevered on the edge of the hill looking down on the water holes where the animals live. It's very comfortable with fax machines and modern equipment. There's an ancillary camp of floating

Dr. Mildred E. Mathias

houseboats called Water Wilderness. Canoes carry eight people to the land where you can walk through the forest and track rhinos. It's exciting because it's a very different view than the one you get riding around in a safari vehicle. Then on to the largest national park, Wankie, where we lived in tree houses and ate outdoors. From there to Victoria Falls, then to the luxury hotel, Chobe Safari Lodge in Botswana, where Liz Taylor married somebody or other. We finished in Moremi Nature Reserve, and the group returned back.

When I went to Windhoek I saw no evidence of segregation in Namibia. In the dining rooms, black people ate at the tables with us. I was really pleasantly surprised at the change, because I had been in Cape Town just at the beginning of apartheid twenty-five years ago, and it was dreadful. At that time I met a South African man who found out I was from the United States and asked, "Why do you hate us so? Why are you so upset?" I tried to explain to that man all the other things that terribly upset me; for example, when I applied for a visa and they wanted to know whether my father and mother were European or non-European. My father and mother are Americans. I knew if I checked non-European I'd be in trouble. My family has been in the United States for several hundred years. To this man, the world had two categories — white and black. Later I met an American woman and joined her for a sight-seeing tour with a Cape Town couple. The guide turned out to be a policeman. He showed us all the new facilities with different platforms for the blacks to get on the train. They had separate windows at the post office. He was proud of it. It was all I could do to keep my mouth shut. Changes have taken place, and I am delighted about it.

I never have any health problems on my trips, and I do keep up to date on tetanus, typhoid, yellow fever [shots]. I always take great quantities of vitamin C, whether I'm traveling or not. In Africa I drink bottled water, but I've discovered that drinking beer is the safer thing. The eighty-five-year-old woman told me she didn't think that she would ever drink beer because she never liked it, yet I turned her into a beer drinker at eighty-five!

Botany is such a broad field. It encompasses all of biology, because if you're in certain fields of botany, you could be working with fruit flies or out looking at the total environment, in which case you need to know the animals.

I set out to be a teacher of science and math at the high school level; there was a shortage of science teachers. My family couldn't afford to send me to graduate school, and in those days there was very little in the way of scholarship or other kinds of support. I would have gone to medical school had it been possible. However, women were not welcome in medical school in those days. If I had had money, I could have bought myself in. In my junior year I was offered support to go on for a master's because of the research I had been doing in the botany field. I made the shift, and my field became botany. I had worked with plants all my life. After the master's, I received a fellowship that gave me the opportunity to continue studying for the next two years.

I came to U.C.L.A. in 1947 in a nonacademic position, in charge of the herbarium. After working a couple of years, I was put on the academic ladder. I already had about forty publications, a research record, and a Ph.D. The garden (now known as Mildred Mathias Gardens at U.C.L.A.), was directed by a representative from the horticulture department and a representative from the botany department. I became its director. This was at the time that U.C.L.A. was beginning to expand its campus at a great rate. We had some real campaigns to prevent the garden from being swallowed up in the expansion. We managed to get an official designation, and I remained director of the garden for quite a period.

We had an estate given by the Vavra family up in Bel Air which had a very fine collection of plants. We started dividing plants in categories and placing identifying labels around the campus. I use the whole campus as a garden when I teach. I know a number of people who have been here really enjoy the garden, and it's often used as a set by people in the movie business. It is the only garden in southern California that is readily accessible to a population of fifty thousand people.

My father was a teacher and a naturalist. My mother was the outdoors person, and was raised on the first ranch in a very special part of the Black Hills in Wyoming. The ranch was willed to the Catholic church. This land has a very special meaning for me. If there was any piece of property that I would like to own, it would be that ranch.

My advice is this: Don't take on a project unless you can fully commit yourself to its completion.

"Don't take on a project unless you can fully commit yourself to its completion."

Lees Meadowcraft

Born in 1899, in Hereford, England, Lees Meadowcraft has worked for Langley Castle for more than twenty years. She began as a gardener at the castle and now works as the senior guide to the estate. Each year, she shows thousands of visitors around the castle's beautiful grounds.

My energy comes from my determination to go on using my mind and my hands. I do believe that activity has kept me from going senile. You have to keep turning your mind over; it's rather like turning over ground, to keep it fertile. Don't just subside into a chair and wait for the next meal. A mental exercise that's been good for me is to go over lines of poetry. I keep going over all the old ones I ever knew, and add to the poems.

Older people have to realize that it's better to do something, *anything*, rather than sit about thinking their knees are bad and their hands don't work.

A lot of responsibilities were pushed at me that I probably haven't wanted. There was my mother to look after, and that did cramp my work. During the Second World War, I wanted to join the Navy very badly, but I couldn't because I had to find a job that also had housing for my mother. Sir William, the owner, asked me to take a job as a land girl in the garden and with flowers. They found me somewhere to live, as well as a place for my mother, so I had no choice but to accept.

Nature and animals are the most important part of my life. I don't think I'm capable of caring for people in the same way as I am for animals and plants. Rescuing some sort of animal from a rotten life and giving it a good home, or growing things and gardening, have given me exquisite pleasure. I had no interest in looking for a boyfriend or getting married. I never wanted a family myself. I've had a lot of dogs and horses to share my life.

I eat very plainly and not more than I have to. I don't eat anything that was ever alive. I don't smoke and very rarely have a drink. I get up at six A.M. and go to bed at seven P.M. I read a lot. I could have done quite well as a jockey. Or probably having been a vet would have been a very satisfying job, but I know also that I would have had to put animals to sleep. I couldn't have done it.

I have enjoyed being a tour guide for Langley Castle.

Burgess Meredith

The American actor Burgess Meredith was born on November 16, 1909. In the late 1920s, he held a variety of jobs, from salesman to reporter to seaman. Mr. Meredith started his acting career in 1930 when he joined Eva La Lallienne's Student Repertory Theater. Mr. Meredith has appeared in dozens of theater, film, and television productions. Some of his more memorable roles have been in **Of Mice and Men** *(1939),* **Advise and Consent** *(1962), television's* **Batman** *series (1966), and the first three* **Rocky** *films. He received an Oscar nomination for* **Rocky I** *in 1976.*

I face myself every so often and I learn that I'm either more depressed than I thought or happier. Life requires stillness and a self-examination from time to time. I do a lot of yoga. Quietness and looking inward help me. It's a necessity from time to time, or else I panic. The accumulation of experience reminds me of building blocks — if you put too many on, they tumble off.

It's difficult to accept the concept of universe without thinking that there's a mind behind it. I have no personal opinion of what God looks like. The rules and law of such things as birth and death in continuum lead

me to think that there must be "somebody there." Sometimes, in silence, in inward introspection, a notion of what "God" is comes over one, but it's nothing you can describe. I have moral standards that I break.

Whenever life has given me a hard time, what kept me going was a kind of pride of not wanting to give in. From the age of eight to thirteen, I was at the Cathedral of Saint John the Divine and I was a choirboy singer. After I left the choir school, I hung around New York and got mixed up with some stealing and other things. I recount it once in a while as a form of penance.

What pleased me most was getting away from my very unhappy childhood into some sort of security. I was born to a broken family and a good deal of desperation and some ill health. It was wonderful to come suddenly out of that to be brought into surroundings that were helpful, protective. Different things have made me happy. For example, in the theater, no performance has made me as fulfilled as when I conceived and directed James Joyce's *Ulysses in Nighttown* thirty years ago.

The nature of growing up is denial; you hide things, not only from other people, but from yourself. Many years ago I was so bound up with the untold areas and stories in my life that I was very severely ill and unable to function. In the early fifties I went to Dr. [Bèla] Michelman, who was very helpful. In his office, I would meet other show biz people, such as Marlon Brando, [Elia] Kazan, and Alan Lerner and others, who felt as I did. We all marched in and out of there, nodded somberly, but always felt better having articulated what was upsetting to us. Suppression and denial are what keep many of us from developing at a certain time of our lives. Writers are more visibly afflicted than other people because they are more specifically articulate than, for example, painters. The things you hide are gen-

erally things that, when they surface, turn out to be not as bad as you thought.

Sharing your life with someone is important. There have been certain wise men who sat on Mount Everest or some mountain in the Far East and shared it only with God, but in the normal thrust of nature, you want to share what you have with other humans.

I am a writer but have not written as much as I wanted. Being an actor has been so easy for me. "My God, you make money yakking somebody else's words!" Zero Mostel used to say.

I would love to have more rigor to accomplish certain things at certain times. As I begin to walk toward the sunset, I know I should be more disciplined about exercising, for example! There is an ongoing battle with myself every morning to exercise. One of my regrets is not to have kept a diary, given my friendship with people like Steinbeck and Thurber as well as many other great people I worked with and got to know so intimately throughout my career.

When I get into feelings of inadequacy or passing depression, I take a tape recorder and speak into it. Some of my best friends are tape recorders.

It's fatigue, the whip of nature, and the gradual lessening of vitality that causes you to "retire." It may be that people in other walks of life retire at a set age, but actors seem to go on. There isn't any time when producers–casting directors can't use an actor who's slightly older. The phone rings less, but you can still go on. Restricting people who are still fully operative professionally merely because retirement law so dictates is not only sad; it's silly and unfair. It's also virtually impossible for people considered over retirement age to start fresh or find other means to earn a living.

Sadness comes when people who might still have something to do can't do it because they've had to work too long, too late in their lives to earn bread and are thrust from their homes. I still have a cup or two of the wine of divine discontent that comes over me, perhaps not as often as I wish. I wish I could light my fuse even hotter. I've never given up thinking that I'm as good as I was. I still have many ideas of what I'd like to do and I am lucky to have the means to try to do them in some tranquility.

"I have a heart full of future plans."

Alwin Nikolais

The world renowned choreographer Alwin Nikolais was born in South-ington, Connecticut, on November 25, 1912. He studied the art of dance from some of the most famous dancers of his youth: Hanya Holm, Martha Graham, and Doris Humphrey. In 1939, he became the director of the Mills School of Dance, while also holding the position of director of dance at the University of Hartford in 1940. In 1946, Mr. Nikolais accepted the position as Hanya Holm's assistant in New York City. He became the director of the Henry Street Playhouse in 1948 and continued in that position until retiring from the company in 1971. He is a master teacher and artistic adviser to the Nikolais and Murray Louis Dance Company.

In addition to choreographing dozens of national and international shows and making tours, Mr. Nikolais has won several honors, including being made a Chevalier de la Légion d'Honneur, Commandeur de l'Ordre des Arts et Lettres in Paris in 1982, and receiving the Kennedy Center Alliance Award in 1987, the American Dance Guild award in 1987, and the National Medal of the Arts, also in 1987.

An artist is always exposing himself to himself; that's really what the function of art is. I've learned to know who I am by watching what it is that I do. I'm always extremely busy. I have a compulsion to change things, which is the prerogative of the artist.

I've done some crazy things. For example, seven years ago, I choreographed a piece called *Scenario*. In his *New York Times* review, Clive Barnes wrote that it was the most vulgar piece of choreography he ever saw. It wasn't vulgar; he just didn't understand it. It was very Italian;

I was dealing with complex emotions. The dancers enacted these emotions and at the very end, silhouettes of their own nudes were projected onto their bodies. I think Clive objected to that. I might not always understand or analyze what I do at the moment I do it, but I've learned to trust myself. The mind is like an eternally running streetcar, and it depends on the moment when you climb on as to what view you'll get from it.

My health regime is work, work, work. I have abundant energy. Unfortunately, too

Alwin Nikolais

much of that energy is used up in the administrative nonsense of the art world today, in fund raising particularly. I have become seventy-five percent fund raiser and twenty-five percent choreographer. While it is imperative for me to fund-raise, I don't particularly enjoy this aspect of my work.

In 1968, I performed for the first time at the Théâtre des Champs Elysées in Paris. Knowing how quick to judge the Parisians are, I was terrified. During the performance, I heard what I perceived to be nasty comments coming from the orchestra as well as the balcony. The curtain came down and there were a few boos in the back, and then all of a sudden, I was overwhelmed by a sudden uproar of bravos. I had been so tense until that point that the release was overwhelming. To celebrate, the French Minister of Culture took us all to Maxim's, where we transformed the place into a disco for the rest of the evening. An unforgettable evening. Since then, however, every time I go back to Paris, I worry that our love affair will stop, but it hasn't happened yet. In fact, when I returned to the Théâtre de la Ville, in my 1988 season, the theater had hung a huge banner saying "Happy Birthday, Mr. Nikolais!" on the outside of the building.

The earlier part of my life took place in the Depression period. I grew up, as most people did, believing that nothing was given to you; you had to work hard to earn a recompense. I was born in a small town near Hartford and had no vision of grand accomplishment. Succeeding in Paris and traveling all over the world has been like living a fairy tale, like flying on Aladdin's magic carpet. My life has been a big love affair with the world. I am an incorrigible optimist. When an event seems to overtake me, I will inevitably rebound and show resilience. I also love to eat good food. I have a light breakfast in the morning, some fruit, toast, and coffee. For lunch, mostly I will have yogurt. And then for dinner, the lid is off. I like to cook!

Hanya Holm, one of the great teachers and choreographers, taught me an invaluable lesson of life. After work, she'd invite us up to have some lunch. Once, her secretary came in and said, "Hanya, there is a leak coming through." We all ran upstairs to see that the water pipe had ruined all of her best photographs beyond repair. We dug them out while Hanya pulled out a bottle of brandy and said, "Nick, always celebrate tragedy; never lament it." If someone has died, celebrate the great things you had together. I have never forgotten that. When I do feel down, I don't stay there.

To me work has always been an activity of pleasure, even if you sometimes agonize when you create. The mayor of Arles, in the course of a celebratory lunch he hosted in my honor, commented on the childlike quality of my work. I don't think of it as childlike, but instead my work reflects, no doubt, an innocence. I work intuitively, mostly. Wallace Stevens once said, "To see again through the eyes of a child," and Picasso, "It took me fifty years to become young." I have a little bit of that in me.

I wish America would grow up a little faster. I do wish the arts could function in the United States not as a special and separate entity, but as an integral part of our culture. Art plays a crucial role in America. When the U.S. is having political difficulties, I am frequently sent to foreign countries as almost a kind of ambassador. Once an ambassador of Panama gave my company a reception after a performance and thanked me, saying, "You don't know how much easier you've made my job."

I don't think that the arts change unless there is some extraordinary outside event that happens and causes them to evolve. In my time, I have witnessed changes, and understand what caused them. For example, at the turn of the century, it wasn't Isadora Duncan who alone caused the attitude toward one's body, and in turn, dance, to change. That transformation was influenced by a multitude of cultural impacts: Freud, Karl Marx, and a signal from the audience, which demanded a new freedom. It wasn't any one artist like Duncan, but a worldwide cultural revolution that caused the arts to move to another plateau. With the explosion of the atom bomb, the world suddenly realized that Einstein was not merely a funny little white-haired science professor with whiskers — his mind changed our concept of time and space. The arts have never been the same since this discovery. We still have the fear of that horror.

I love people, and I love to teach. My students are my investments, because they are the ones who will shape the future. To be involved with their lives is very gratifying.

"My life has been a big love affair with the world."

Frances Freeborn Pauley

Frances Freeborn Pauley was born in 1905. She is a registered lobbyist with the Georgia State Legislature. In the 1960s, Frances Pauley became very involved with the Civil Rights movement, working for the Office of Civil Rights and the Georgia Council on Human Relations. Later, she went on to form the Georgia Poverty Rights Organization. Currently, she devotes a great deal of her time to working with the Atlanta Interfaith AIDS Network and serves as the chairwoman for People for Urban Justice.

The people I've worked with since I turned seventy-five have broadened my life. I think I've learned more in the past two years than I ever learned in my whole life put together.

In 1940 I started working in the Capitol. I'm a registered, unpaid lobbyist. Sometimes I lobby just as a citizen . . . and sometimes I sign in under one of the organizations I work with. The primary lobbying I have done in the last years was to obtain money for AIDS research and patients.

As you get old, your eyesight dims, you seek hearing aids, you can't even taste and smell as you once did — but the pain and anguish in seeing people suffer seems to increase. I simply have to think of some new arguments, some new ways to make the general public understand and help instead of continually blaming the victim.

I've been working on the AIDS Hotline and I'm writing a book about an eighty-four-year-old woman's first day on an AIDS Hotline —

her heartaches, pain and also the extent of her devotion, love, and compassion with which she comes — I come — in contact. That's the only beautiful side that the AIDS epidemic has brought.

During the Depression, there were many children who didn't have a nickel to come to the show or buy a hotdog. Hearing about a federal hot lunch program in the making, I called up all the principals in the county to a meeting. And within six weeks we had hot lunches in our county. I also worked in the League of Women Voters during the time when the Supreme Court passed a ruling to desegregate the schools. It was at that time that I realized how little I knew about the African Americans who lived around me and decided to learn more about their world. I began working in the Civil Rights movement in 1960. With the Georgia Council on Human Relations, I helped to organize interracial groups which worked to bring the two races together. For five years I worked with the Office of Civil

Frances Freeborn Pauley

Rights on the federal level as the coordinator for the State of Mississippi. It took a while to be cleared for a Civil Service job because I was sixty-two years old. Later, I organized a new group called the Georgia Poverty Rights Organization, made up of poor people and welfare mothers. My participation in all of these struggles for justice has taught me compassion.

My working day varies. I work entirely from home. I have recently moved with my computer to an efficiency apartment in a home for the elderly. About a hundred and fifty of my friends got together and bought me a computer for my eightieth birthday.

Currently, I'm the chairwoman for People for Urban Justice, a coalition that works against the practices of the labor pools without any regulations. Often we find virtual slave markets. The merchants and businesses are shamelessly making money off the backs of the poor. We're trying for reform. On the board are lawyers as well as homeless people themselves. The homeless are some of the most beautiful people I've ever met. When people think of homeless, they think of bums, drug addicts, and drunks. But in fact, the homeless population is a cross-section. Since I have more political background than anyone else in the group, when a bill needs to be introduced, I am the one who knows how to get it passed. I'm also working on a metropolitan AIDS interfaith network. Everyone on the board is a rabbi or a minister except me. We have just opened a new day center for children with AIDS.

My advice for young people is to work hard. You might often wonder if you're going to sink. You may not always be successful, but it doesn't matter. So much of what I considered a failure at the time, I now realize was a step toward success. Do what you want to do. If you want to grow roses, grow roses. If you want to tend babies, tend babies.

I got married during the Depression. Instead of being able to go on with the theater, I was just working to take care of my family. My father, my brother, and my husband, two children, a few dogs and cats, all lived together; despite the difficult times we had an awful lot of fun together.

Einstein said solitude was painful when you are young but delicious when you are old. Sharing my life was important, but today, I find a lot of beautiful things about living alone.

My father taught me that "if you can't say something good about somebody, don't say anything at all." I try and live by that but I do enjoy a little ugly gossip occasionally.

The racial situation has come a long way. But we have a very long way to go yet.

As for my health, I have check-ups and watch my blood pressure and diet to some extent. I'm too fat, but it sure is hard to lose weight when you like to eat. There's so much work to do. Stress gets in the way. I'm more forgetful than I used to be. I'm deteriorating, but I'm determined to keep my schedule and do my work as well as I possibly can. The more you think about yourself, the worse shape you get into. And the more you think about your fellow man, the better off you are.

My kids are now age fifty-six and fifty-nine. And there's nothing that makes me happier than to look in their faces, to see that they're happy, leading useful lives, and know that their kids are all thriving.

My husband died five years ago. He always encouraged me to be independent. For my generation, that was unusual. When he died, I sat down and made myself a schedule to fill the emptiness — volunteer work with the ACLU, the Poverty Rights office, and generally thinking and helping others.

A dozen bad bills were introduced in the legislature this last session discriminating against the gay community. It's so divided now, the open gays and the closet gays, and they dislike each other. It reminds me of the '60s when the black community was divided, the NAACP not liking the SCLC. Because I have no emotional attachments, I can talk more easily with a homophobic legislator than a gay man can.

One night I was out late in a slum area of the city, and I stopped at a light and a car drove up right by me. I looked over there, and here were two big black burly men. The window turned down real fast and he yelled out, "Frances Pauley, what are you doing here at this time of night? Don't you know this isn't safe? Do you want a ride home?"

"I've learned more in the past two years than I ever learned in my whole life put together."

Milton Petrie

Milton Petrie was born on August 5, 1902, in Salt Lake City, Utah. Mr. Petrie, a legendary business tycoon, is the chairman, president, and chief executive officer of the Petrie Stores Corporation, a national retail clothing company. A well-known philanthropist, Mr. Petrie is particularly interested in helping policemen and their families in addition to families who have been the victims of violence.

I don't feel any different at age eighty-seven than when I was forty. Older people can have a great influence on our society, and this later period can be extremely fulfilling. I'm healthy and energetic. I go to work every morning at eight-thirty A.M. and take care of my business.

I inherited my energy and drive from my mother. From her I learned that to get ahead you have to work hard, ignore the clock, and always challenge yourself. I graduated from high school and couldn't afford college. Early on I decided to get out of poverty. When I first started in the business, I must have worked twenty-four hours a day. You have to be tenacious and have a bit of luck to keep going strong.

I made a lot of mistakes in my business career, and I even went into bankruptcy. But I managed to pay all my creditors. And then after quite a struggle, I came right back. We've got now fifteen hundred and seventy-one stores and did over a billion dollars of business last year. I started Petrie Stores Inc. in 1927 with five thousand dollars. Shows what you can do in America.

My greatest pleasure in life is to help people in need. I also have a special affinity for policemen and firemen; my father was a policeman.

There was a time that I didn't like myself. I was a very heavy drinker and, in fact, an alcoholic. I joined Alcoholics Anonymous in 1941, when I was thirty-nine, and when they were just getting started with no more than two thousand members. Today AA must have about two billion members. I can't say enough about the wonderful things AA does.

I was born in Salt Lake City. My father had several pawnshops, and he went broke. My mother foolishly persuaded him to leave Salt Lake City because she was ashamed of the stigma. If he hadn't, he could have made a comeback.

They left and went to Indiana, and he opened up a little shop there. He went broke again. Fortunately he had a rich sister, who got him a job on the police force. For the next twelve years he was a policeman until he retired. I'm very proud of that.

I scan the papers and listen to the news and am always alert for people in trouble. I know what it's like to be poor. My parents wanted me to be a decent person, and encouraged me to do what I could for humanity.

I read in the paper that Anthony Venditti was gunned down by mobsters and his widow, Pat, was left with four girls to raise on a small pension. I send her twenty thousand dollars each year, and I set up a college trust fund for each daughter. Also, I help Steve MacDonald, who is in a wheelchair for life, and his children. I've done the same thing for others, and I intend to continue.

I smoke cigars. I take a little red pill, a Theragran, every morning.

I've got a great rapport with my three children. And for the past twelve years I've had a wonderful life with my wife, Carol. Man cannot live alone.

People don't realize what you get through giving. For me, nothing is more rewarding than helping others.

Dilys Powell

*The famed British film critic Dilys Powell was born in 1901. After graduating from Oxford University, she joined the **Sunday Times** as a staff writer in 1928. In 1939, she became the film critic for the **Sunday Times**, and held that position until 1976, when she began to review television programs for the paper. In 1979 Dilys Powell became **Punch's** film critic and she continues to review for the magazine today, as well as contributing pieces to the **Sunday Times**.*

*Dilys Powell has written several books, among them **Descent from Parnassus** (1934), **Remember Greece** (1941), **An Affair of the Heart** (1957), and **The Villa Ariadne** (1973). In 1984, she received the BAFTA Award of Honour.*

What really matters to me is endurance. I often get very tired at my age and think, "I can't get up this morning" or "I really can't do this." But if I didn't have work, I'd end up unfocused and unmotivated, and that would be absolutely appalling. While I know that one should be thinking about others, I can only be preoccupied about myself. How to survive until half past four this afternoon or to tomorrow is my main concern these days.

My work really makes me happy. In my writing, I often feel nothing is ever as good as it should be, but it nonetheless gives me great pleasure. Writing is a painful pleasure. I'm more critical of my writing now. In the past, I would read something I had written and think,

Dilys Powell

"That's not too bad." I've learnt more and, with age, one grows less satisfied with one's work and one's own personal behavior.

I've had two happy marriages. My first husband was an archaeologist. He died in 1936. We had only been married ten years. I was very fortunate later to meet, at the *Sunday Times*, a fellow journalist, who also happened to be my boss. We were married very happily for twenty years. He was very encouraging to me and I learnt a great deal from him. It's so important to be with someone who knows and understands what you're doing. I feel sorry for people who don't really care about anybody very much and don't share. Sharing your life is the most important and lucky thing. When someone you love dies, immerse yourself in work and friendship; it is the only way to survive.

Writing is a very painful pleasure. In the middle of it you often tell yourself, "I can't do it; I can't think of anything to say." Do struggle on.

I receive mail from people who tell me they are grateful for my work. Their gratitude always surprises me, since my writing emanates from a personal need.

I don't really mind being older; however, not being able to do things I used to do bothers me. Particularly now, because I can't walk. I broke my hip and so I totter about with my dog and rely on taxis since I can hardly get on a bus. Being unable to travel anymore is a reminder of my old age. While you're barred from a good many pleasures, there are always other compensations. With age, you have more confidence in yourself. What other people think or say about you seems less important. You also understand people better. You can't help learning something in eighty-nine years.

My parents weren't intellectuals at all. From them I learned the rules of decent behavior. I was brought up in peace and love.

I don't really do anything about my health. Thank goodness, I feel well most of the time.

My grandmother might be responsible for my early vocation as a writer in that she encouraged me at an early age even in my silly childish attempts. I began as a journalist with the *Sunday Times* writing book reviews.

I happened to be in the office when the job of film critic for the *Sunday Times* fell vacant, and I was given the job. Being there at the right time was my good fortune. I started reviewing films in 1939, the year the war broke out. I still write for them as well as for "Film of the Week" for television and *Punch*.

For a young person wanting to become a film critic, I should first recommend learning everything there is about the cinema. Watch a film not once but four, five times and try to see what it is about it which excites or moves or appalls you.

For me, contemporary cinema is becoming too violent. I often wonder whether these films don't actually encourage violence. I look back on cinema, which was then so simple, and in a way, so pure. Perhaps we shall get over this period of violence and overintellectualism. Cinema is a reflection of the world in which we are living.

I remind myself that cinema is an art. I'm just a critic, yes, but art — if cinema is that — will transcend criticism.

Going Strong

"What really matters is endurance."

Marcella Rabwin

Marcella Rabwin was born on May 15, 1908, in Richmond, Virginia. After graduating from the University of California, Los Angeles, she became the assistant to the film mogul David Selznick, working on such films as **Gone With the Wind.** *After working with Mr. Selznick for some twenty-five years, she became an active civic worker in Beverly Hills and Los Angeles.*

Marcella Rabwin currently resides in San Diego, California, and writes for various magazines.

There is nothing to life without the life of the mind. To sit in a rocking chair, unless you're completely crippled, is a sin. I don't want any rocking chair in my life. We will all go into oblivion if we don't keep thinking and keep working. And so I've dedicated myself to learning and creating. Creativity and joie de vivre are important. Rubinstein at ninety-two was still recording. When my life has been difficult, willpower kept me going. My background has bred strength in me. I had to work, raised four children, and had a very successful marriage. I also had a serious career in the community. I took care of myself; I put myself through college by reading for English teachers. And during the holidays I worked as a telephone operator.

The happiest times of my life were certainly not during my career — that was a strenuous time — but instead, during my marriage to a very brilliant surgeon who was chief of staff at his hospital. I married in the midst of my career a man selected for me by my bosses — David and Irene Selznick — who were both very fond of me. I worked for David Selznick for about fifteen years, as his executive assistant. After meeting a young doctor, he thought, "That's a great guy for Marcella." I had been going out with charming young actors, directors, and writers at MGM but six weeks after meeting the penniless doctor, I married him. I continued working with Mr. Selznick for a few more years. Eventually those late hours in the projection room got to be more than my husband could take. We adopted four lovely children. The sum total of my fifty-four married years was one great big, long, happy time, and I have to be very grateful for that.

A life lived alone is a life of selfishness. The love of my husband, of my children, and certainly of my good friends, has been a lifesaver for me.

I graduated from U.C.L.A. and went to work at Bullock's. From there to Warner Brothers and eventually I became Darryl Zanuck's secretary. Subsequently I became an agent. After earning a great deal of money, I quit because the male agents didn't like a lady's competition. When Mr. Selznick took over the RKO studio, I joined him. From his office I quickly moved upward.

After leaving Mr. Selznick, I worked for the community, building the library in Beverly Hills and arranging the bond issue. I also in-

217

Marcella Rabwin

fluenced the city council to buy Greystone for the AFI. All of these things were accomplished by getting up at five A.M.

I had my little office donated by Nate and Al's. I went in there at five-thirty A.M. and got all of my good hard work done before nine A.M. I could then start my telephoning. I'd stay there until late in the evening, then I'd go home to my husband and children.

Working for Selznick was difficult. Yet I worshipped David O. Selznick. He was a man for all time as far as movies were concerned, but a merciless man when it came to the numbers of hours he demanded of his people. He also thought nothing of making them wait hours for him. He was the most brilliant producer. He made some of the great classics like *Anna Karenina, David Copperfield, Tom Sawyer, Dinner at Eight,* and *Intermezzo.* With *Gone With the Wind* we were in a bind. Selznick was a perfectionist and a genius. We spent three years trying to cast the picture. Today you would hire a casting director. We had two characters who had to be exactly what we thought the fans expected. And one of them was Clark Gable — we had a very difficult time getting him, and in the end it cost Mr. Selznick's half of the picture. We had to give up half of it to MGM in order to acquire this man who did not want to do the role. Clark Gable was married and trying to get a divorce to marry Carole Lombard. And part of the deal was that Metro would give his wife, Rhea Gable, one hundred and fifty thousand dollars if she would divorce Clark. He would then be able to play the part. We didn't yet have our Scarlett O'Hara. The best of the local film tests was Paulette Goddard. The picture had started, and Mr. Selznick told Paulette, "You bring me a marriage license and you can have the part." She was presumably married to Charles Chaplin at the time. Despite the fact that she had agreed, she couldn't come up with the marriage license.

Mr. Selznick's reasons were that the people in the South would never have accepted a woman living with a man openly. When we finally signed Vivien Leigh, she was living with Larry Olivier. We had to separate them, and rent two houses.

My work now is completely new and an unexpected twist in my life. Now I spend most of my time writing. It keeps me young. I enjoy selling what I write. I get up in the morning and go straight to my typewriter. I'm about to venture onto something very difficult — buying a word processor — and I am terrified.

I write until lunchtime, then take a rest. I read my morning's work at lunch. I go back about two-thirty and I stay until five P.M. I have a worldwide correspondence with friends and an enormous fan mail correspondence because I am the last executive connection to *Gone With the Wind.*

I won't submit an article where I don't think it will be accepted. I know where to send them and, as a consequence, I never have a rejection.

Recently a car hit me broadside and propelled me into a very large van. I was trapped to the neck. They had to cut me out and hauled me off to the trauma unit at U.C.S.D., where they saved my life. But I was comatose for about three days with three broken vertebrae, a broken arm, foot, and leg. Almost every inch of my body was broken or bruised. I stayed in the hospital for weeks. Then I was in a wheelchair. And now I'm running all over the place. It was a terrible accident. And you wouldn't expect an eighty-one-year-old woman to recover from such a traumatic experience.

I was determined to make it, though. The mind has a great controlling force over the physical body.

I take a nice little bunch of vitamins. I eat very sensibly. I had a stroke twenty years ago.

Going Strong

My husband wanted me to get out of this community because he felt that they're going to bill me.

I miss my husband, but I appreciate friends. I know I have to keep on living. I go to the theater, to the ballet, and the opera. I have season tickets to everything in San Diego.

My symptoms of aging are a little arthritis, which is certainly normal. I had high blood pressure, and I have little TIAs, sort of minor strokes, a couple of times a year. It manifests in a little weakness in the arms; stuttering really is the tipoff to it. My good doctors take pretty good care of me. I'm interested in clothes, I keep my hair and my nails in good condition. I have an apartment that's all decorated in red, which is certainly not the color of an old lady's place. I had a heart attack last year. And three weeks after, I took my ten-year-old grandson to Africa. I was determined not to break the child's heart. I read three newspapers every day. And I look at all the best things on television. I've been many times around the world. And I plan to continue.

"I've been many times around the world. And I plan to continue."

Margaret Ramsey

Margaret Ramsey has been the agent for such British authors as Robert Bolt, Joe Orton, Alan Ayckbourn, Peter Nichols, John Arden, David Hare, and Christopher Hampton. She is held in such high regard by her peers that she was awarded the Industry Award by the British Film Institute — an award that usually goes to cinematographers and film editors.

Curiously, I do have a kind of morality, which, as I perceive it, is for me what God is. I have this sense that there is a reason for behaving honorably. I don't know how one gets a sense of morality. It would be nice to believe in God. When you grow nearer to death, somehow you think about morality.

I don't think I'm introspective. I wish I'd had ambition; my way of thinking "I'll just live and see what turns up" crushed any possibility of ambition. I have just allowed life to live me, really. I would have liked to control life.

My mother tended to doubt me. When I became an agent, she never believed that I really had meetings with some rather famous people. She wanted to control me and wanted me to be a nobody.

It would have been better to have a definite chosen career instead of merely drifting into being an agent. I never wanted to be an agent. And I don't quite remember how it happened.

Life is really wide open. I try to help my clients. I wouldn't allow them to be treated badly. I don't ever wish for people to make false statements about my clients. What holds me to the agency is the clients, the people. Money is not the issue.

When life is giving you a hard time, try to endure and live through it. You must never run away from a problem. Convince yourself that you will survive and get to the other side.

I arrive in my office in the morning at ten and meet with writers. I'll talk about their work with them on the phone, and then they'll come in and we'll discuss it some more if they wish. I try not to impose anything. I merely suggest things to writers.

I don't have friendships with authors because I feel that one mustn't ask anything of them. Being an agent is providing a service for them, but as such you don't necessarily expect to enter their lives. You can't expect them to be your friends. If it happens, that's lovely.

I avoid doctors. I keep healthy by eating fruits and vegetables rather than meat. I drink but never get drunk. Both my father and brothers are doctors. If I could restart my life, I'd be a homeopathic doctor.

I would say simply to young people, "Dare go over the top." I mean, "Don't stop yourself. Dare to go beyond anything that you think you should go."

André Gide had something I liked at the end of one of his books: "All I can say to my reader is — throw the book away."

Ronald Reagan

Ronald Reagan was born in Tampico, Illinois, on February 6, 1911. President Reagan began his professional career as a broadcaster for the Chicago Cubs. In 1937 he moved to Hollywood and made his screen debut. While in Hollywood he was elected President of the Screen Actors' Guild. From 1967 to 1974 he served as Governor of California. He became the fortieth President of the United States in 1981, and was re-elected for a second term in 1984. Presently, President Reagan has an office in Los Angeles, where he lives with his wife, Nancy, and spends the weekends on his horse-breeding and cattle ranch in California.

Starting at the beginning, we were a family of four — mother, father, and a brother two years my senior. My brother and I never had any grandparents, as they were all in the place up yonder before we were born. One thing was drilled into us from the time we were old enough to understand. It was that prejudice and discrimination — racial or religious — was a cardinal sin. We both still feel that way.

Our mother was devoutly religious and the kindest human being I've ever known. We were on the edge of poverty, but she could always find someone worse off than us and provide needed help.

Nelle, my mother, taught us that if something went wrong, something made us very unhappy, we should take it in stride and not let it get us down. She promised that down the line something good would happen and we'd find ourselves realizing it wouldn't have happened had that other unhappy thing not taken place. I can point to a dozen or more happenings in my life that have proved her correct.

But enough ancient history. She instilled in me a faith in the power of prayer, a belief in the goodness of humankind and that God does look after us. I understand what Lincoln meant when he said (while he was President) that he "couldn't meet the responsibilities of that position for a day if [he] could not call upon One who was stronger and wiser than all others."

I also took as gospel the statement of someone unknown to me that "a gentleman always says and does the kindest thing." Now don't get me wrong — I'm not trying to paint myself in saintly colors. I'm telling you what I know and believe is right but like all humans, I don't always toe the line. I don't know if I can ever deserve all the good things that have come my way, but I'll keep trying.

Dr. Daniel Reeves

Dr. Daniel Reeves, born in 1915, is a chiropractic doctor and a healer. He began his career as an attorney for the federal government. In 1973, he retired from law to practice chiropractic and healing full time. He also has a Doctor of Divinity degree from the Fellowship of Universal Guidance. His office is in Glendale, California.

My force comes from tapping into the energy that is all around us and just letting it flow through me into the patients. I view myself as merely a conduit to accomplish the result I want. It started out in the '50s. I was in a scientific research group observing the power of prayer on plants. We would take twenty corn seeds, put them in two piles, alternately, using identical methods for growing. We would pray over one pile and ignore the other. Three days later, we measured the shoots and the roots. The ones we prayed over were longer.

From that point on, I became interested in healing. I became involved in a Japanese form of noncontact healing called *johrei*. The johrei people drew energy through a little amulet that they wore around their necks. We were taught to have that amulet inside our heads. For me, that amulet was a picture of the human Christ. So I drew that energy through my head and would project it through my hands to the person I was working on. Later, we found that it was much more powerful to use contact with the hands on the skin. I could feel the energy flowing through me. The more I work, the more it flows. The more sensitive I become, the stronger the flow of energy.

In the '50s, I was working with the government as a lawyer. I became interested and studied various healing and metaphysical groups in my spare time. In a counseling session I was told to take up chiropractic so I would have a legal right to do what spirit had qualified me to do. I worked from seven-thirty A.M. 'til four P.M. daily and went to chiropractic college five-thirty to eleven at night, Monday through Friday. I studied on the buses and on the weekends. I got my license and built up a practice at night and on weekends and made plans to retire as a lawyer. My boss died, and I had to make serious decisions: to stay on and become district counsel, retire from law, or become a full-time chiropractor. I opted for the latter. I have never regretted it.

I eventually bought my own office. "Going strong" for me represents being interested in and enjoying the work that I do as well as continuing to learn to improve my skills.

Out of my original healing group, an organization was formed: the Fellowship of Universal Guidance. The teachings that were channeled through that organization have given me the background to not only study myself, but also to help people with emotional problems. It was a concept which is known as the "three selves evaluation." At the time the teachings were coming through, they seemed entirely new to us and we had no knowledge of the *huna* work at the time.

Huna is the Hawaiian mystical religion. And the practitioners of that mystical religion were known as Kahunas. They were healers and teachers and priests. As the teachings developed, people familiar with the huna work said what was coming though was very similar to the writings by Max Freedom Long.

Through the study of these books — *Secret Science Behind Miracles, The Secret Science at*

Dr. Daniel Reeves

Work — it was possible to compare the psychological concepts that we have received from Freud and from Jung with other new learnings, making it possible to study ourselves.

We all have multiple subpersonalities which develop around a particular activity. Sometimes, it is the subpersonality we may not be particularly proud about. At other times, we are, because of the uplifting feeling we have when that subpersonality is present and doing the work.

The work that I am doing now is the most gratifying of my lifetime. There have been high points in my career, but none come up to the satisfaction of the results of working on patients now. We all live by the law of "as you sow, so shall you reap," the law of karma. I feel we are here to learn and to experience growth, and everything we do adds to that experience. I engage in a number of different activities, and I feel that I grow from each one. The most growth that I'm achieving in this lifetime is coming through the healing aspect. And the longer I do the healing, the more satisfaction I get.

When I'm working with the patient, I always am conscious that I am not the one that is doing the work. I am merely the physical extension of a group of entities who are working with me on the other side of the veil and, although I don't see or hear them, I do sense them. Some of my clairvoyant patients can see those who work with me. But I have not developed that ability. This said, I sense their presence and I am in telepathic communication with them, especially with Edgar Cayce. When there is a particular problem, I will check with Edgar Cayce and see what telepathic ideas he projects to me. Some of the things I do may seem quite unorthodox and hard to explain until the results appear.

Whatever you do, have faith in its efficacy and take every opportunity that you can for it to be reinforced. If you have no faith in what you are doing, it will block any success that might be coming your way.

As I studied metaphysics before I took up chiropractic, I had a good understanding of karma and realized that nothing happens by chance, and I feel that the teachings I have received through the Fellowship of Universal Guidance have been a great benefit in shaping my religious and philosophical beliefs.

From my parents I had an oral knowledge of the Bible. Sometimes patients question whether there is any reference to the Bible in my work. I refer them to the twelfth chapter of First Corinthians, which speaks of the gifts of spirit and therein is a mention of the gifts of healing, among others. The thirteenth chapter of First Corinthians is the great chapter on love. If we are going to be a success, we have to be cognizant of that.

I received my legal degree in 1939, my A.B. and J.D. from the University of Cincinnati. Then I went into World War II and became a combat engineer unit commander in Europe. Eleven months of combat from D-plus-one on through V.E.-Day, and then we were ordered to reassemble for training for the invasion of Japan.

As I became more interested in metaphysics, I realized that God is much greater than anything that we could ascribe to an anthropomorphic god. I view God as being everything. In God we live and move and have our being. And in each of us is a spark of God that I view as being sent out from God to experience many different forms of experiences. I feel there is a duality in each of us, and it is through our choices between good and evil that we are able to experience and to grow.

I used to be very secretive about what I did, especially when I worked for the federal government. I didn't want people to know my full metaphysical background because it could have prevented me from achieving district counsel if people thought I was a metaphysical kook. I had to be conventional and, even though I started out as a healer and added chiropractic to the healing, I hid the use of healing behind the facade of chiropractic — although I used energy in my chiropractic practice rather than force. Now my practice is oriented to practically all metaphysical patients who fully understand what I do.

One word of advice for anyone going into healing is to be very aware of the need for protection. When you are working with energies, you can remove negative energies from someone. These negative energies can lodge in you and destroy your effectiveness.

Prior to going to bed, clear out the negative events of the day. Do not take any negativity into the sleep state with you. Before going to sleep, and if I wake up at night, I use the mantra protection from the Fellowship of Universal Guidance. I use it between patients to clear out any negativity that I may have picked up from them. I also make it a practice to wash my hands with sea salt and water between patients. This, too, helps me clear out any negativity that might still be with me from the previous patient.

"The work that I am doing now is the most gratifying of my lifetime."

Pascal Regan

Pascal Regan was born in 1914. As a young girl, she studied sculpture in Italy and painting in Paris. She returned to work and live in Los Angeles, where she continues to paint and sculpt. Her art can be admired in many private collections and museums throughout the world.

The title of this book is what it's all about. Live life, strongly, to its full potential. I don't care whether you're in a wheelchair, on crutches, or in a bed; give whatever you can — intellectually and mentally. Age means nothing. If age had something to do with it, would my husband, who is eight years my junior, have married me? For your own personal happiness, don't let age get in your way; it's the biggest stumbling block you'll ever have. It'll be a hurdle you'll never get over. At seventy-six I'm only getting started. I can't imagine not working. It's just as important to me as eating and breathing.

I was lucky not to have been aware of my handicap. I was deaf until I was eighteen, when I underwent four surgeries because of congenital malformation of my left ear. While I was able to receive some sound, it was not enough to speak, so I could not go to school.

My mother would communicate with me by drawing — and with other people I enjoyed doing the same, so everything that I did was what was before my eyes and my hand. My mother encouraged me in everything; she made me feel everything was possible. I have seen mothers destroy their children when they could have become really extraordinary people. Their parents put them down and they were never lifted up.

My mother's sister was married to an Italian and I went alone with him to Italy. He lived with his big family in a farmhouse outside of Rome. The barn was a studio of a sculptor and teacher, Professor [Antonio] Utillio. I started sculpting, but because I was not optically good in reduction, I'd see things in subtraction, and modeling is addition. They thought I'd be better as a painter. Other artists used this barn and then, by chance, one man brought this

Pascal Regan

piece of soapstone to carve. I asked whether he would let me work with it. They gave me a piece of soapstone and I seemed to show an aptitude. I stayed eight years. I wasn't lonely because I had something to do with my hands.

I don't think about myself very much, and I never have. Starting when I was eleven and a half, I developed tunnel vision, and I didn't have time to look inward. I was looking outward all the time, at whatever I was creating.

When I got my hearing back, I wanted to paint. So I went to Paris, where I studied for years, but I longed to get back to sculpture. Talent is a combination of sweat — and dedication. I can't wait to get up in the morning to see what's happened and what I left the day before. I never know, because in a different light, it's another way. I divide my day between painting and sculpting.

I am extremely religious and a Catholic. I think religions are all alike, basically. Before I start any piece I bless myself. I don't think any of us do anything totally alone. And I rely on this feeling that there is someone helping me. It may be in part because I lived alone in a silent world and my communication was something that I didn't understand.

Every day, except for Saturdays (I like one day off), I walk with my husband to church. Mass is a very nice time to be quiet and collect myself. They don't give sermons on weekdays, so no one intrudes on your thoughts. My husband is a retired Catholic monsignor. I met him at my daughter's wedding. I don't really know if he gave it up for me, or if he would have anyway. He's a very brilliant man, speaks five languages, and I have learned so much from him. He makes me better than I am. We've been married twenty years this month.

Time is very precious. My old teacher told me that the main thing is to learn to be lonely and to say no. I've never been lonely, but I have a hell of a time saying no. When you're always alone in your studio, you need to go out — I become very gregarious. For twelve hours I don't talk to anyone except when I have lunch with my husband.

I think most people are born with a germ of creativity. You have to develop it. But not enough people are willing to work and really sweat.

The most important happiness is to be loved and return that love.

When you've lived to my age, seventy-six, you've picked up a few ideas along the way. I've married a few times; two of my husbands died. People who live alone become very selfish. I don't think people have to be creative, but if they don't get involved and give of themselves, they turn inward and become totally absorbed in self.

If we go on holiday, I always carry an easel with me. On vacations, we'll stop the car and I'll go out and paint. Then I'm totally happy again. If you've worked from the age of eleven to seventy-six, you're pretty much into a formula. These days, I usually wake at six A.M., work from eight-thirty to six P.M., with an hour for lunch. I try to go to bed early.

Everyone has to have something to do, whether it's physical, or whether it's just giving your time, reading to the sick, or looking after some children. In a sense, scrubbing the floor is a work of art. Do something physical — do the best you can.

I really believe age can be determined by the age of your health. I've seen people in wheelchairs, paraplegics who manage to do something with their lives. I do believe that no matter what handicap comes your way, you can live with it, get used to it, and use it.

I had one very hard time when I was married to a man who was up for mail fraud. The FBI and the IRS as well as the police grilled me. I was going to lose my house. I had already lost my money, and everything had gone down the tube. Here I was, fifty years old, never been broke before, and suddenly I had tremendous bills to pay in order to get my house back. I lived in fear, in a house without lights. I would go to bed at night, and my legs would be numb. It was a very dire time. But, however bad things are, if you keep a positive attitude and keep busy, you will break through all the misery. It's not a good idea to sit down and bemoan what's happening to you. During that rough period, I worked harder, and that was the best thing for me. If some kind of a scandal hits you, people more or less avoid you.

For future young painters or sculptors, if you're really dedicated, paint every day. Even if you hold a job, every evening try painting. That's the main thing. They say, "How did you become so successful?" I reply, "I walked the streets of New York with my portfolio and had a thousand doors slammed in my face." I had to go to Europe to make it.

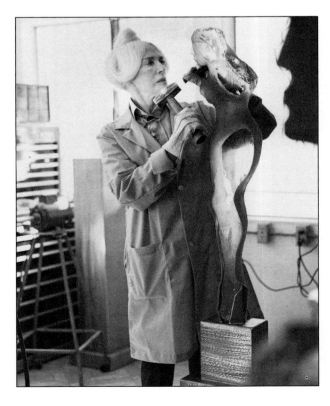

"Live life, strongly, to its full potential."

The Honourable
Miriam Louisa Rothschild

Miriam Rothschild, born in 1908, is a naturalist well known for her research on fleas. She has contributed more than 280 articles about the insect to scientific journals. From childhood she has had a passionate interest in flowers, butterflies, astronomy, and the weather. The many books she has written include **Catalogue Rothschild Collection of Fleas,** *volumes I (1953) through VI (1983),* **Butterfly Cooing Like a Dove** *(1989), and* **Dear Lord Rothschild,** *her biography of her grandfather, in 1983.*

It is very important in old age to keep an interest in one's work. If you're lucky enough to combine work and pleasure, as in my case — what I call "work" is really pursuing my own interests — I see no reason why you shouldn't go on 'til you're a hundred.

My father was called the inventor of modern conservation, and the subject has always attracted me. He was the first person to realize it wasn't the rare species you had to conserve, but the habitat in which they lived. This was his great contribution to the concept of present-day conservation. When one is young, this type of activity may not appeal to you as much as research and the discovery of exciting new facts about nature. But when you get older and see wild flowers disappearing because they are drained and weeded, and sprayed out of the countryside, or wantonly destroyed, you realize the importance of conservation — that now is the perfect time and opportunity for you to work for their survival.

The pleasures of old age really depend on your health. If you're lucky and you're pretty fit, it can be both enjoyable and amusing. Don't regret too much that your eyesight and hearing isn't as good as it was, or that when you jump over a gate you haven't got any spring left in your knees! Because I am a naturalist, I find it is interesting to observe the changes that take place with age. For example, I had above-average eyesight when I was young and took terrible advantage of it by doing too many long hours at the microscope. Now I'm over eighty, I notice the different ways in which your eyesight varies as you get older. You lose your spectacles or forget where you put them. But then, even if they're on the table in front of you, and you look and you don't see them — this is because there is something wrong with the way your eyes focus. Accommodation is one problem; another is perception: even when you actually *see* the thing, your mind doesn't always take it in and appreciate it as quickly as in the past. You immediately appreciate the difference in, say, a bird's eyesight when he is looking for a moth, and yours — particularly with insects which have to conceal themselves from predators from birth. As you get older you can compare the various ways in which your eyesight begins to fail and then modify your daily life to meet these new problems.

When I was young I was the most unself-conscious person that ever lived — which is probably the reason I am supposed to be eccentric and why I ignore fashion: Even now I am preoccupied with the outside natural world.

Perhaps happiness can be divided into two different compartments. I can say, without any

The Honourable Miriam Louisa Rothschild

hesitation, that I've had the most sustained enjoyment out of my children. I was absolutely enchanted with them right from the day they were born. My family always came first. But apart from them, my main interest has been the natural world. The mountains are what I've liked the best and mountain scenery and all the natural history of the mountains. Mountain air is wonderful. And time in the mountains seems quite different to anywhere else. It's the most exhilarating and incredible experience to watch dawn at high altitudes and to hear the dawn chorus of the alpine birds — which begins before you really see any light. It's like little bells tinkling in the rocks. Another part of the world I loved was the South Seas. I can quite understand why the explorer Captain Cook dallied there. Because once you're there, you can't imagine why you need be anywhere else! The climate is strange, and it has this effect on you. Initially I went to Tahiti, Mooréa, and various other islands in the South Seas merely to study butterflies, but I discovered they had a magic of their own when I had only been there for a few days.

My father was a scientist — he was a flea specialist — as well as a naturalist. I grew up in this world of natural history and it was second nature to me. One of my earliest memories — at five years old — was collecting ladybirds. I was a very precocious naturalist and was already able to sort these beetles into different species. I believe that naturalists are born and not made. My astute father instantly realized this and he gave me live mice as pets — not dolls to play with. He put a butterfly net in my hand and taught me all I knew, up to the age of fifteen, about natural history. My mother had a much greater influence on the other aspects of my education — my great love of children and family life.

I was fantastically lucky in having marvelous parents. Never at any moment in my life did I have a disagreement or rift with them, never a quarrel or a bad moment — unthinkable the idea that I would ever be punished. That's a wonderful start in life.

I have a long working day. I get up at five A.M., cook my own breakfast, and then I go out to my animals to continue my scientific experiments. I'm studying the faculty of memory in my birds — its development and improvement. At half past six I talk to the farm manager about the day's work on the farm. I go round the garden, have a look at how the wild flowers are getting along, and often, if a few cut flowers are needed for the inside of the house, I select them, cut them, and take them home to arrange. And at eight o'clock people appear from the village and bring the post. Then I deal with my letters until nine o'clock. I have a very voluminous mail, consisting chiefly of scientific correspondence and letters about conservation and growing wild flowers. People ask to see the fields or to buy seeds or plants, or they may need advice on how to grow them. Frequently gardeners with small plots want a wildlife corner. At nine o'clock my secretary arrives. We discuss the mail and other matters. At ten o'clock I do a round of the gardens and work with the gardener or collect data in the nature reserve. Then I settle down at my desk to do my scientific work, which means reading, writing, and thinking. And that carries me on through the day.

As a concession to old age, I've been advised by everybody I respect to rest after lunch; otherwise you don't do much good work in the afternoon. So between one and two P.M., after a midday snack, I watch television, which sends me to sleep almost instantly. After a forty-minute snooze, I go back to my desk and work solidly on until about five P.M. with one interruption, when I go back to the gardens to do the memory experiments with my birds for the second time.

Going Strong

I had to give up microscopy because I caught shingles of the eyes. Shingles is the elderly person's version of chicken pox. Although my vision is all right — so I can't complain — it is not good enough for close work with a microscope.

My first interest was marine biology. After my marriage it was impossible to continue this line of research, as we lived a long way from the sea. So I changed to entomology and studied insects, especially fleas. It was a subject suitable to do at home. I only worked in the evening, because of my six young children. I was once looking down a microscope and my son Charles, a young baby at the time, was screaming his head off. And I said, very irritably, "Just for once why can't someone feed that child?" quite forgetting he was breast-fed. This tale was always told against me — I don't know if it was really true.

I never set out in life to do anything with a definite objective. I just did what came along — what really interested me. I was passionate about natural history and discovering new facets about the insects I came across. I think I was lucky not to go to school, and I never passed a public examination.

I had a very old governess who used to teach me about the Romans. And we only read Walter Scott. I was self-taught, and my surroundings in the country were ideal and there were natural history books everywhere. When I was fifteen, my father died, and for two years I abandoned natural history. Then I went to Chelsea Polytechnic and took evening classes there and learned a little conventional zoology.

If you want to take up biology as a career, I would advise young people to get a certain amount of straightforward academic learning, and thus acquire a sound basis in botany, zoology, and some chemistry. Afterwards you can go out into the fields, and watch and listen.

I've never had a health regime, but I do try to have a reasonable diet. My whole family tend to put on weight. When I was young, I was too thin. But when I got older, and after I had children, I had a tendency to become too fat. I try to limit what I eat — not too much fat or sugar, although I do love chocolate and eggs. I have taken a lot of exercise in my life — perhaps too much — and thoroughly enjoyed all sport like skiing, riding, and squash.

If I have a religion, I would say it is goodwill — something you really should try and cultivate, and hopefully find this quality in other people. I also believe you can persuade others to appreciate nature, and anybody who really becomes interested is truly lucky. It is something that lasts.

I have recently become involved in wild flower cultivation, and at first I found it very depressing that it takes years to restore wild flowers to the countryside, yet you can destroy them very rapidly. Governments are usually in office for periods of five years, and consequently they never think it worth their while to take long-term views about anything. If you're considering conservation, you must think in hundreds of years. And one of the most distressing things for a conservationist to face is the fact that short-term big business always wins. You stand back and have to witness the environment wrecked and destroyed before your eyes. I suppose we have to recognize that man is a successful but greedy species and he'll always go out for a short-term gain.

But I feel one can be optimistic about the Greens. That's the great achievement of the moment — people have suddenly woken up and realized they are destroying the planet. When I was young, nobody thought about it. This is a tremendous step forward. Eventually one will succeed, but it's bound to be a slow and difficult process.

C. A. Scott

The newspaper owner Cornelius Adolphus Scott was born in Edwards, Mississippi, on February 8, 1909. He attended Morehouse College and the University of Kansas. In 1934, Mr. Scott helped found the **Atlanta Daily World,** *the longest-running black newspaper in the nation, which he still manages.*

My creativity is fueled by a belief that God intended everyone to be free and able to develop according to the talents they were given.

What has kept me going is Christianity. . . .

I've always tried to practice being patient and considerate of the rights of others. I treat people like I want to be treated.

I was fortunate to have had the example of fine parents. My father taught us little boys to follow the big boys, and all the boys were supposed to support the girls. He inculcated those principles in all of us.

My family went into printing because we felt we could do more to make the Constitution a realistic document by being printers and running a newspaper than by being ministers. Lawyers and doctors are not protected by the Supreme Court. It's just the church and the free press. We believed, as young men, that we could better solve the race problems, which were big at that time. They extended the whole length of the South. There was no education. I have no resentment about that. All races — Chinese, Japanese — have experienced prejudice, but, as young men, we un-

C. A. Scott

derstood the concept of this big Constitution.

Our newspapers, the *Atlanta Daily World*, the *Birmingham World*, and the *Memphis World* — started the editorial policy of pursuing the blacks' right to vote, and the most gratifying thing in my lifetime was winning that right for my people in the Democratic white primary.

This is the only great continent on earth where there's a large number of black and white people living together day and night.

I was a Roosevelt Democrat from 1932 to 1952 until the election of the immortal Dwight D. Eisenhower, whom our paper supported. He effectively challenged the great problem of race and segregation.

If we can live in peace, as black and white Americans, despite our problems, we will go forward and become the hope of mankind.

Lincoln, a common lawyer, never went to church, but behaved like a Christian. He said this country couldn't survive and endure with people half-slave and half-free. The emphasis on the need to eliminate slavery was put into motion.

Work to do a job well, not just to get paid. Make sure what you're doing will help others. My father's motto was "Be sure you're right, then go ahead."

I came from a close-knit family, and there was no temptation to lie. I was taught in school about George Washington and the cherry tree and it stuck with me.

My parents were married in 1900 in Kentucky and then went on to Mississippi. My father became a leader of the Knights of Pythias, a black Masonic lodge. He had a theological degree and wanted to preach. My mother was a great Christian woman, and her grandfather was an American Indian.

My father bought a little printing office in 1901. There were only two or three printing offices in the whole state of Mississippi run by blacks at that time. He hired a young man who taught my mother how to print. Because my father was a minister, he needed a printing shop to print his manuscripts and little sermons. They also did commercial printing. That was the beginning.

I came along as the fifth child in 1908. I learned how to print when I was six years old. I was inspired by my first sight of a linotype machine. It's one of the great inventions of the world. It changed education and revolutionized history. Years ago we set the type letter-by-letter. My momma and I would set type by hand. I had a true passion for it.

I got my inspiration to be somebody right on this street in Atlanta. My oldest brother, W. H., our founder of the paper, who called me "Bobcat," said, "I want you to go to Atlanta. We're going to own us a printing office and in a receivership we can buy and start a newspaper."

Our family newspaper, the *Atlanta Daily World*, was started in 1928 and is the oldest black daily publication in the United States. Out of it grew the *Birmingham World* in 1930 and the *Memphis World* in 1931. In 1932 the *World* established the Christmas Cheer Fund, and it has continued annually to give to the needy.

When I was young I didn't have a timetable for success. I worked and did the best I could with common sense. I survived and made constant strides. We had been running a semi-weekly. In 1931 it became a triweekly. Then I went to Kansas to get my training in journalism. Kansas was the first state in the West that didn't have slaves.

Adversity develops a man. If everything's smooth with nothing to think about but enjoying yourself, you won't do much thinking. Necessity makes you think. I know it helped me.

Going Strong

"Adversity develops a man. If everything's smooth with nothing to think about but enjoying yourself, you won't do much thinking."

Nicolas Slonimsky

Nicolas Slonimsky, born in 1894 in St. Petersburg, Russia, came to the United States in 1923 to lead an accomplished musical life as a pianist, composer, pioneering conductor, and musical lexicographer. He's conducted major orchestras all over the world, including ones in Berlin, Paris, Budapest, and San Francisco. Highly respected for his work as a musical lexicographer, he edited **Baker's Biographical Dictionary of Musicians.** *In addition he's written* **Music Since 1900** *(4th edition, 1971),* **Music of Latin America** *(4th edition, 1972), his autobiography,* **Perfect Pitch** *(1988), and* **The Lectionary of Music** *(1990).*

I have had four careers: as a pianist, a writer, a composer, and as a conductor. In my family, to be creative and energetic was normal. Everyone was exceptional. It was stressful, and eventually led me to thoughts of suicide.

I am never satisfied about anything I do, except perhaps after some of my lectures or occasionally after getting a very nice write-up from people I esteem. My sense of humor is the only thing I like in me. Right now I am working on a book whose title is *Thirteen Uneasy Lessons on How to Become an Intellectual.*

When I was sixteen, I worked with a girl at a silent movie theater. One night as we were working, she kissed me on the back of my neck. This sent me into ecstasy and I was too bewildered and happy to utter a word. I remember her name — Katia — to this day. I recorded the whole event in my diary, which my mother read. She asked me, "Nicholas, do you know what syphilis is?" She continued, "If you let Katia kiss you again, you'll get it and your brain will turn to jelly." "I'd be perfectly willing to have syphilis if only she'd kiss me again," I thought. For months I dreamed of Katia.

I was the oldest person to make a London debut as a pianist at ninety-five years old. The Central TV Company in Birmingham made a documentary of me. Usually I can't stand looking at myself, but this time I found it very amusing. The title of the show was "Nicolas Slonimsky, a Genius, More or Less."

My father and mother were remarkable. My father was an economist and a writer and the first to write a book in Russian on Karl Marx, in 1890. Lenin was twenty years old at the time, and it is said that apparently, upon reading my father's book, he decided to become a Marxist.

One-third of the entire population of St. Petersburg died of famine and diphtheria in one year. I didn't. But I often had nightmares about it. I gave music lessons and was paid a quarter-pound of black bread for each lesson.

My cat doesn't believe that I am anything special until I show consideration for her, by getting out of bed and feeding her. I have recorded my story in my book *Perfect Pitch.* It begins with the sentence "When I was six years old, my mother told me I was a genius." The rest of the book is devoted to the refutation of this notion.

HAVENWOOD-HERITAGE HEIGHTS
JULY 13, 2008 – JULY 19, 2008

Day	Time	Activity	Time	Activity
Sun. 7/13	8:00am	Church Bus (H) 8:05am (HH)	10:00am	Buddhist Group- Chapel (H)
	8:30am	Church Bus (H) 8:35am (HH)	11:30am	Sunday Brunch – DR 1&2 (HH)
	9:00am	Church Bus (H) 9:05am (HH)	3:00pm	Vespers –Auditorium (H)
	10:00am	Church Bus (HH) 10:05am (H)	4:00pm	Vespers –Chapel (HH)
Mon. 7/14	7-9am	C.H. Lab Draw – Hav. Home Health	10:30am	Gentle Tai Chi – DR3 (HH)
	8:30am	Armchair Exercise – DR3 (HH)	1:00pm	Grounds Committee – Art Rm (HH)
	8:30am	Gentle Yoga – Audi (H)	1:15pm	Duplicate Bridge – DR3 (HH)
	9:00am	Energy Study Group – Conf Rm (HH)	2:15pm	Monday Program - Auditorium (H)
	9:00am	Exercise – Auditorium (H)		Elderhostel Introductory Presentation
	9:00am	Aerobics w/ video – DR3 (HH)	4:00pm	Croquet Playing – Croquet Court (HH)
	9:30am	Quilting Group – Sewing Room (H)	6:30pm	Wii Playing – Conf Rm(HH)
	9:30am	Armchair Exercises-LAL (H)	7:00pm	Sing A Long – Chapel (HH)
Tues. 7/15	7:30-9am	C.H. Lab Draw – HH Home Health	1:00pm	Downtown Bus from (HH)
	9:30am–11:30am	Home Health Office Open (HH)	1-2pm	Fitness Instruction – Fitness Rm. (HH)
	9:30am	Quilting Group – Sewing Room (HH)	11:30pm	Bingo – LAL (H)
	9:30am	Downtown Bus from (H)	2:00pm	Billiards for Fun – Billiards Room. (H)
	10:00am	Tuesdays at Ten – Chapel (HH)	3:30pm	Healing Services – Chapel (H)
	11-12pm	Fitness Instruction – Fitness Room (H)		**DINERS CLUB – CHEN YANY LI**
	12:00pm	500 Area Strawberry Festival	4:30pm	Pick up begins at H then to HH
	12:30pm	Blood Pressure – Home Health Ofc. (H)	6:45pm	Game Night – Coffee Shop (HH)
Wed. 7/16	7-9am	C.H. Lab Draw – Hav. Home Health	10:30am	Episcopal Eucharist – Chapel (H)
	8:30am	Armchair Exercise – DR3 (HH)	10:30am	Gentle Yoga – DR3 (HH)
	9:00am	Exercise – Auditorium (H)		**TRIP – CURRIER GALLERY & LUNCH**
	9:00am	Aerobics w/ video – DR3 (HH)	10:50am	Bus pick up at H, 11:00am P/U at HH
	9:30am	Crafts – Sewing Room (HH)	1-2pm	Fitness Instruction – Fitness Rm. (HH)
	9:30am	Men's Chat –Café (H)	1:15pm	Scrabble, Whist, etc. – Deli (HH)
	9:30am	NO Sign Chi Do – Audi (H)	1:30pm	Group Meditation – Chapel (HH)
	10:00am	Circle of Friends – Great Room (H)	3:30pm	Chapel – Chapel (H)
Thur. 7/17	7:30-9am	C.H. Lab Draw – HH Home Health	11-12pm	Fitness Instruction – Fitness Rm. (H)
	9:30am–11:30am	Home Health Office Open (HH)	12:30pm	Blood Pressure –Home Health Ofc. (H)
	8:30am	Men's Coffee Chat – DR2 (HH)	1-2pm	Fitness Instruction – Fitness Rm. (H)
	9:30am	Downtown Bus (HH)	1:00pm	Downtown Bus (H)
	9:30am	Armchair Exercises- LAL (H)	1:00pm	Theater Workshop – Chapel (HH)
	10:00am	Computer Club – Happenz (H)	2:15pm	Movie "America's Wilderness"- LAL (H)
	10:00am	Clown Workshop – DR3 (HH)	3:00pm	Billiards for Fun- Billiards Room (H)
	10:00am	Art For Fun – Art Room (HH)	6:30pm	Evening of Music – Great Rm (H)
	10:45am	Line Dancing – Activity Rm (H)	6:45pm	Game Night – Deli (HH)
Fri. 7/18	7-9am	C.H. Lab Draw – Hav. Home Health	10:00am	World Concerns- DR 3 (HH)
	8:30am	Armchair Exercise - DR3 (HH)	1:00pm	Cribbage – DR1 (HH)
	8:30am	Gentle Yoga – Audi (H)	1:00pm	Knitting Group – Sewing Room (HH)
	9:00am	Exercise Class – Auditorium (H)	1to3pm	Popcorn Day – Café (H)
	9:00am	Aerobics w/ video – DR3 (HH)	1-2pm	Fitness Instruction – Fitness Rm. (HH)
	9:30am	Knitting Group – Sew Rm (H)	1:30pm	Assorted Games – LAL (H)
	9:30am	Mall Bus from H	2to4pm	Popcorn Day – Coffee Shop (HH)
	9:40am	Mall Bus from HH	3:00pm	Billiards for Fun- Billiards Room (H)
	10:00am	Trivia – Apple Court (H)	4:00pm	Croquet Playing – Croquet Court (HH)
	10:00am	Artist's Studio – Art Room (HH)		**NEW HAMPSHIRE MUSIC FESTIVAL**
			5:45pm	Bus pick up time for H, 5:55pm P/U HH
Sat. 7/19	10:00am	Wii Playing – Conf Rm (HH)	2:00pm	Emma's Tea – Café Extension (H)
	11:30-1	Deli Service (HH)	2:15pm	Movie, "Three Comrades"- LAL (H)
	1:15pm	Afternoon Bridge – DR3 (HH)		

Demystifying Your Cable Bill
By Michael A. Palmieri, President/CEO

Did you know that Havenwood-Heritage Heights has a special cable deal with Comcast? For many years HHH has purchased bulk cable services from Comcast and this allows us to charge you a very low monthly rate of $16.50 per month for basic cable services. So, this week we'll focus on cable bills and how they interrelate with a Comcast bill.

Your cable fee from Havenwood-Heritage Heights appears on your monthly statement in the amount of $16.50 which represents a special bulk rate. This rate is significantly discounted compared to those in homes outside of the Havenwood-Heritage Heights community.

If you want any additional cable services from Comcast, you should contact them directly. These additional services will vary in price based upon what you desire.

Comcast does have specific additional charges for things like: high speed Broadband for computers, premium channel packages, high definition cable boxes, etc. All would appear on a separate bill to you from Comcast.

If you ever have a question about your bill, even one from Comcast, we are happy to look at it on your behalf and we simply ask that you photocopy it for us.

✦ We at Havenwood-Heritage Heights know the Comcast representatives and can always seek clarification on your questions.

Sidney Smith

The British gardener Sidney Smith was born on January 7, 1915, in Ashford, Kent. As a young man, his first job was at Thomas Farm, where he learned all aspects of farm work. He later moved to Carter's Seeds in Watford. Mr. Smith is currently gardener at Redsell's Farm.

I've learnt two things in my life: godliness and cleanliness. We used to go to church every day, because if you didn't, your father wasn't allowed to have any eggs from the farm. And so with thirteen of us in the family to feed, we all had to go. You marry for life. I've had a wonderful married life with Kathleen for fifty-three years. And I always believe in share and share alike. We brought the children up to do the same, and both are good children. I have an older sister of ninety-six. There's only two of us still living, from the thirteen.

I've lived a fulfilled life. Once you start retiring and sit about, you're going to die. Your whole life drifts away from you, and you've got nothing to look forward to. I had a healthy brother who always worked on a farm. His wife said, "Now we've retired, we're going to relax and not do any more." He was dead within six months.

When I get up in the morning at six, I take the dog for a walk and the wife a cup of tea. Then I come up to this garden that I love at eight A.M., work 'til noon, come back again one to four, and then I come home and have my tea and then I usually go work in my garden.

Just keep going. If you're in a flat and you've got no gardening, do some sort of sport.

All I do for relaxation is go fishing. I go one day a month and just sit and fish.

You can apply gardening to any form of life.

My father was a wagoner on the farm; that's a horseman. And all the time he was around I never really swore. His salary was fifteen shillings a week. At four in the morning he'd go and see to his horses, come back, have his breakfast, and then he'd go to work all day 'til six o'clock at night, six days a week — and he had to look after the horses as well on Sundays.

Fifteen shillings a week, thirteen children. And two lodgers.

It was a happy family. When I was thirteen years old, the schoolmaster was going to cane my sister for some reason. So I gave him a hiding. And because of this I had to leave school. Tom, a farmer where my father worked, went to the school cause I had to go to Borstal — the reform school — for hittin' the master. He took me away and told them I'd work for him and live with his family for twelve months, with no pay. Then I was clear. I lived better there than what I would have done if I was at home. When he died, he left me twenty-five pounds. Which them days was like a hundred. He was so good. He really cared for me.

I don't believe in dieting. I've been out in the open air most of my life. I've only had one illness, and that was two years ago. My heart missed a beat. I had a weekend in the hospital and they couldn't find out what was wrong with me so they sent me home. It did frighten me.

I don't think there's anything I don't eat. My best meal is a beef pudding made in a cloth. You don't get that today. I've always eaten terrifically fat meat. I can't bear lean meat. I do like butter; I don't want this imitation. I go to bed at midnight.

When I first started on this farm — forty-five years ago — there were a hundred and thirty men working. Now there's six. Sir Thomas Nieman had the best-kept farm in Kent for two years running. People was conscientious in them days. With all the money you're getting you could push money to the shop on a wheelbarrow, that don't buy happiness, does it?

Dr. Robert Wallis

Robert Wallis, born in 1900, is an internist, painter, physicist, and a pioneer in the fields of time and pulsed magnetic-wave research. Born in Paris, he moved to the United States in 1940 and has practiced here since then. Dr. Wallis is a member of numerous medical societies and lectures all over the world. He is considered to be one of today's foremost lecturers in the field of internal medicine, and his articles have appeared in over fifty medical journals.

Activity is the basis of my health and happiness, activity in every shape and form — physical, artistic, scientific, and sentimental. I rode a motorcycle until I was eighty years old. Riding my motorcycle gave me the impression of independence like nothing else did. My energy originates from my constant curiosity, enthusiasm, and incentive. Enthusiasm comes from the Greek words *en theon,* meaning "God in yourself."

What we do not do is as important as what we do. I tried in my younger years to follow the Golden Rule of Pythagoras, the rule of three eights — eight hours to work, eight hours to sleep, eight hours for everything else. Of course, I cheat, and normally I follow the rule of the four sixes — twelve hours to work, six hours to sleep, and six hours for everything else.

I've always had a strict diet. I eat like a beautiful woman who wants to keep thin. I follow my instinctive appetite. I don't drink, except for nonsparkling mineral water, and I eat fruit before each meal. My regime is very simple: I take a little of everything and much of nothing.

People forget that when you're sixty, you need fifty percent less calories than when you're twenty-five. This means that if you eat the same amount (assuming that you exercise as much, which is never true), you are eating too much. Then you put a stress on the organs

Dr. Robert Wallis

of elimination — the liver, the kidneys, the intestine — and to defend yourself you make fat, which is dangerous. Now when you are eighty, you need about seventy-five percent less of the calories that you needed when you were twenty-five. Naturally, when you reduce the quantity you must improve the quality.

I do believe that aging is a deficiency disease. As we age, we absorb nutrients with less efficiency. Therefore, we must give our digestive tract the opportunity to make up for the lack of absorption. Everyone has a different capability of absorbing, and thus we must compensate for this failure. Treatment has to be personalized. You might lack certain vitamins, minerals, or glandular products during different moments in your life, and each prescription must be tailored to compensate for the deficiency in order to help nature on its own path.

It's better not to take mixed vitamins at the same time, but to take separately, for example, vitamin C and pure vitamin E. I do believe that the complexes of minerals and vitamins are no good, because vitamins are very sensitive and are destroyed by the minerals. There are many experiences that I could report that prove this very well. Take them separately and personalize them and see what is necessary.

I do believe that if we die before eighty, unless it's an accident or a tumor, we kill ourselves by overeating, overdrinking, oversmoking, and underresting. After that it's in the hands of God. There is an old French saying: "Si jeunesse savait; si vieillesse pouvait" (If youth knew; if old age could). This being said, I do believe that chronological age doesn't count. What counts is biological age and how you feel.

I get up at seven o'clock. After gymnastics, a shower, and a short breakfast, I go into the office. I read several newspapers, and at nine I start seeing patients.

I read five evenings out of seven. I read mostly scientific magazines of physics, medicine, also literature and politics. Given the type of research I do, there is little time left to read books.

I do my painting on the weekends. Lately, though, I have taken more extensive weekends with Roxanne Wehrhan, who has been my friend, close associate, and disciple for thirteen years. We frequently go to the country, where I live the life of a gentleman farmer: cutting and stacking wood, mowing the lawn, following the seasons. I try to keep in perfect muscular shape. Twice a week, to maintain my suppleness and agility, I have a Japanese masseur give me shiatsu. Shiatsu is excellent.

In my medical practice I've studied and applied pulsed cold magnetic waves for many years with great success, never losing interest in my early work as a physicist at the Pasteur Institute. I also use ordinary magnets of different strengths extensively. Magnetic waves, whether pulsed or continuous, can help tremendously in a number of cases: e.g., in reducing pain, helping to cure certain infections, and in accelerating the consolidation of fractures. This is really the medicine of the twenty-first century.

Life is an electrical phenomenon. Over thirty years ago I brought this knowledge to my research on personal time, a question that has preoccupied me all of my life. Not the time of the stars or of our watches but the functional time of our brains and lives. In 1964 I published a pioneering book called *Time, Fourth Dimension of the Mind,* in which I demonstrated that this type of time is an electrical process that is connected with the function of our electronic computer-brain. And from there I attempted to show that it could well account not only for all the modalities of our physiologic behavior but also for its variations in neurosis and psychosis. When the electrical current stops, our time in all senses has run out.

Going Strong

My exposure to and understanding of the fragility of life has not made me timid. We die only once. Hard times are normal. There are no ups without downs. Accept it. I do believe that one has to have daily contemplation, a moment of meditation. You must always dedicate half of the time to consider, to ask, and to investigate, and the other half to receive the answer, even if it comes from yourself or heaven.

Never forget who you are. This is a whole attitude that is very important. Do not lie to yourself, and if you do, take the responsibilities of your action. People are not responsible enough today. They seem to have lost the moral conscience of which the Bible speaks.

Taking into account the tendency of the administration to overwhelm and supervise everything, I would tell young people not to start medicine now. However, if you really have a passion, keep it alive. Today's system of Medicare and socialized medicine interferes with a doctor's freedom. Their work is increasingly denounced as "unnecessary" by laymen who know nothing of medicine or the patient. This impairs a doctor's performance. Time is lost and research crippled.

Medicine has changed character. I am a survivor of the type of medicine that I practice, which is general medicine. General medicine, or internal medicine, has become a specialty. Specialists are justified when there is a special technique required. However, there is no such thing really as a specialist of the heart or the kidney or the liver, because these organs are part of the overall picture. I tend to endorse the American definition of specialists: "People who know more and more about less and less." As you can see, I am against medicine's trend toward specialization and bureaucratic authority.

I came to America on September 9, 1940. Having dealt with atomic energy, I could not stay in Europe any longer. Ambassador William Bullitt knew that I was persona non grata with the Germans and was aware of the fact that I had dealt with heavy water. I was part of the team that was instrumental in removing it from Norway and giving it to the British and the Americans. My sponsors at that time were Ernest Hemingway, who was the godfather of two of my children, and President Roosevelt himself, who gave orders to grant me an immigration visa immediately.

I'm accustomed to thinking on my feet. Therefore I can answer any question. If I don't know, I will say, "I don't know." All my life, I have practiced the virtue of ignorance. I always knew the limit of my knowledge, and I was always curious to go further and to ask questions and to investigate. That is why I have always been an avid reader and thinker. To be creative, you have to confess your own ignorance and always search to go further.

Robert Wise

The film director and producer Robert Wise was born in Winchester, Indiana, on September 10, 1914. He began his career in films in 1933 when he joined RKO as a staff cutter. In 1943, he became a director with 20th Century–Fox, later moving to MGM in 1949.

Two of Wise's most loved films are **West Side Story** *(1961), for which he won Academy Awards for Best Director (with Jerome Robbins) and Best Picture, and* **The Sound of Music** *(1965), which also earned Academy Awards for Best Picture and Best Director. Other successful films include* **The Body Snatchers** *(1945),* **The Day the Earth Stood Still** *(1951),* **The Desert Rats** *(1953),* **Run Silent, Run Deep** *(1958), and* **The Andromeda Strain** *(1971).*

"Whatever you do, don't ever retire. That's the end," my father advised. I've been active and most of my friends are the same. I enjoy my work — my filmmaking — and my family and my life just as much now, if not more perhaps, as I did early on. For people who have any thought of retiring or wonder what one does in one's older age, this book will show just how fulfilling life can be in the later years of one's life.

I'm from a small agricultural town in Indiana. I went to a school near Indianapolis called Franklin College, where I intended to major in journalism. I had no idea of being in film, as

Krāsaina amerikāņu mūzikāla filma
Цветной американский музыкальный фильм

MŪZIKAS
SKAŅAS
ЗВУКИ
МУЗЫКИ

Robert Wise

this was before film schools were very prominent and part of college education. It was the mid-Depression, 1933, and I had to drop out of college after one year because there was no more money. I couldn't get a job. I had an older brother who had the wanderlust and had gone to California five years before. He got a job at RKO studios, on a labor gang, and worked his way up by 1933 to the time office and the accounting office. With the very bleak and dim future, my family sent me away saying, "You go to Los Angeles with your brother, get a job, and earn a living." The fact that he was working in the studios was my big break. He got me an appointment after a couple of weeks with the head of the film editing department, who needed a young kid with a strong back and a weak mind, I guess, to carry prints of pictures up to the projectionist for the executives to look at. That was my start and my break. I started off to be a journalist and ended up a filmmaker.

My mother was very close to us and was most concerned about the children getting as much education as possible. She did a lot of extracurricular work to allow me to go to school. My mother was by far the biggest influence; she was always very supportive.

I bounced right in from film editing, over a weekend, to directing a film, and started as a young, very nervous director. Since then I have learned to calm down and take things in stride. Whether in my filmmaking and directing, as well as other aspects of life, I have learned to give a lot of thought and preparation to everything. The results are always better.

The most joy in my life has come from my film career, starting as a film editor, working with Orson Welles on *Citizen Kane,* and then going on to direct my own. Filmmaking is very fulfilling, very challenging and a great learning experience. A number of my films have been accepted by widespread audiences, as well as by critics and the Academy. That has been stimulating and exciting. I've won four Academy Awards, two for directing and two for producing the best picture of the year. The enormous international success of *The Sound of Music* has given me great reward. Wherever I go, when people find out I have done *The Sound of Music,* I hear, "That's my favorite film." When my grandchildren come over, they always insist that that's one of the films they must see.

I was married for thirty-three years to my first wife. She unfortunately passed on fourteen years ago. I married Millicent Franklin in 1977. It's very important to be able to have one's own very personal and intimate life, along with a life out in the world.

If there are problems, I face them and lay them on the table. I have found it much better to be very direct and very honest.

We all hit rough times. To overcome whatever the problem is, you have to believe in your own strength and your own ability. You have to believe that you can do it, because you know that you have done it in the past. There is no need to be cocky, but don't forget your self-worth.

Over the years I have watched my diet carefully. The foods my wife and I eat are free of preservatives. I exercise; I walk a couple of miles every morning. You function better if you are healthy and not burdened by too much food or too much weight. Preventive medicine is something I strongly believe in.

From 1980 on, I was on the Council of the National Network for the Arts for six years. I was president of the Director's Guild from 1970 to 1974, and president of the Academy from 1985 to 1987. That took up a lot of time. I was kept very busy with these organizations. I also continue to develop scripts. I believe it's very important to keep an office if you possibly can. It gives you a focus.

To a budding filmmaker I say get your foot in the door any way you can. You can't start at the top but with perseverance and endless determination, you'll climb.

"Whatever you do, don't ever retire. That's the end."

Beatrice Wood

Beatrice Wood, born in 1893, is an artist and potter who was closely associated with the Dadaist movement. Both Marcel Duchamp and Henri-Pierre Roché were her teachers, close friends, and inspirations. With worldwide clientele, she is an internationally acclaimed ceramic artist. Her studio and house are in Ojai Valley, California.

I've learned to be able to say "no," which is the most important word in the English language, certainly for women.

Sixty-three years ago I became a member of the Theosophical Society. Its precept is that you believe in the unity and the brotherhood of the human race. It's not a religion. Arabs, Presbyterians, Mormons, anybody can be a Theosophist. We are all the same. When I went to Japan and India on an official visit, I didn't know anything about their protocol, so I decided to be myself. It seemed easy meeting people that way.

If I am still going strong, it's because I feel I still have so much more to accomplish. My working day begins the night before at one A.M. In bed I review and prepare what must be done the next day. I do it according to numbers. Number one, at seven-thirty A.M. I rush into the workroom, in my nightgown, and get work started. Around ten-thirty, my beloved secretary, Stephanie, arrives. A little later, wonderful Singh comes and we have conferences. There are telephone calls to take care of, letters to answer, and visitors to see. Sometimes, I manage to get a little clay work done

Beatrice Wood

during the day, but not often. Then at night, after a dinner on a tray at six-thirty while I watch the news, I go into my workroom and work 'til eleven. One of the great gifts of being old: one doesn't need as much sleep. I get into bed around one A.M., read a little bit, and by the time I fall asleep, it must be one-thirty to two, and generally I wake at seven-thirty A.M.

Because I never have time to shop, I often order things from catalogues; I also have such fun when the parcels arrive. I've not given up romance.

It's vital to share your life. There's polarity, duality. And if there's love, it's marvelous. I'm not in synch with today's world because I don't believe in promiscuity.

Hardships and handicaps can be a blessing. Because they stimulate our energy to survive them. You'll find if you study the lives of people who've accomplished things, it's often been done with the help of great willpower in overcoming this and that. I loved my beautiful mother, but she was impossible. She wanted me to be social, and that was not in my being. She interfered with everything I wanted to do. I was brought up very conventionally, while underneath there was something in me that always revolted. I went on the stage to earn money so I could run away from home. For two years, I was the ingenue at the National French Theatre. My mother insisted a maid go with me and sit in the makeup room. The actors naturally hated me because she always insisted I play star roles. And she never allowed me to even look at a man. I finally jumped off the fence into a great well of burning oil and learned what life was about. I was burned but I did learn. I had an exhilarating sense of freedom and knew where I wanted to go.

Desire is a mischief maker. When we're completely free of any kind of desire, I think the will to live ceases.

I feel physically free, living in a house that I like, choosing my own friends and my own work, in this beautiful old high valley, looking at mountains every day of my life.

Pottery as a career happened to me rather slowly. I'd become interested in painting. I had the great luck and privilege in my early twenties of meeting Marcel Duchamp. He invited me to draw in his studio whenever I could get away from home. He and his close friend Henri-Pierre Roché encouraged me to draw. Drawing and painting became my life. One day, in the thirties, I discovered clay and managed to make two little figures. It was the height of the Depression. When somebody bought them for two dollars and a half, I felt very encouraged. I made others, and they too were bought. I subsequently took a class at U.S.C. A whole new field of possibility with clay opened up for me. Pottery became my new life.

The moment Marcel Duchamp and I met we started a romance. He was an extraordinary person, much more so than his paintings. He really was a Zen priest: very free, very generous and very intelligent. Later, when I met his friend Roché, the walls of Jericho fell; Roché broke my heart. He [Duchamp] and Roché were very close friends; they both loved me, and I loved both of them at the same time. It was a wonderful relationship with no jealousy. Both men were concerned about educating me, bringing me into reality away from my dream world. I did learn. And I'm very proud of being able to run my own business.

For young people going into pottery, my advice is to learn the technical aspect of pottery. If you want to be mass-produced, that's one thing, but if you take the artistic route, as I did, go to museums, look at great pottery, get books and magazines with beautiful pictures, and let this play on your eyes, on your senses. Deliver when promised. It is important to learn the importance of bookkeeping as well as the capacity for hard work. Having a sense of professional responsibility is very important.

I indulge in a little bit of milk chocolate after luncheon and after dinner. It peps me up. Otherwise, I'm a very small eater and a vegetarian. I take milk every day, and sometimes I also have a nap.

The fact of being ninety-seven years old impresses others. Not me. I don't feel my age at all. I'm very hard of hearing. But I have learned to accept it.

I do have a private secret. Every night after my household has gone to bed, around two in the morning, through my back door Harry floats in to spend the night with me. And Harry is wonderful. He comforts me if I'm lonely. He tells me I'm wonderful and must not be discouraged. He hugs me. And then at six-thirty, he floats out again. Nobody ever sees him. He is the ideal man who remains in my life.

There are three precepts by which I live. The first one is "Now"; it's the present we must be focusing on. The second one is "Shit"; nothing really matters with time. And the third is "I do not know." Because the moment one thinks he knows, the mind becomes closed. Those three precepts are going to be on my tombstone.

"The fact of being ninety-seven years old impresses others. Not me."

My thanks go to everyone who helped make this book possible,
especially Ed Victor, Andy French, Jane Donahue,
and Jeannette and Dick Seaver, who are both my publishers and
inspired editors. I would also like to thank my husband,
Michael, for carrying my camera bag and for his constant loving support.